The Art of
WESTERN RIDING

Suzanne Norton Jones
Foreword by Jimmy Williams

Schooling photography by Tom Masamori
Drawings by Jean Shawbinger
Editorial Assistance: Mary Leslie

Cover model – Jodi L. Smith
Cover photography – David Smith

Melvin Powers
WILSHIRE BOOK COMPANY
12015 Sherman Road
No. Hollywood, California 91605

—— Library of Congress Catalog Number 66-19683 ——

Printed in United States of America

ISBN 0-87980-273-1

FOREWORD

A thorough and comprehensive book covering western riding has long been needed. Finally, a qualified horsewoman has undertaken the task.

Suzanne has used her many years of experience in this field to clearly impart to the reader her basic methods of instructing rider and horse. Suzanne's riding and teaching has not only been limited to the western saddle. She is equally proficient as a rider of hunters, jumpers and basic dressage. The latter, I believe, may have had some influence on the outlines of the excellent "Arena Tests' 'to be found in this book.

THE ART OF WESTERN RIDING systematically covers phases in instruction, training and showing, as well as judging. In addition, it contains illustrations and explanations of equipment, plus an up to date coverage of the American Horse Shows Association rules.

As in all books of this type, there may be points on which people will disagree. However, I feel that THE ART OF WESTERN RIDING is a most helpful guide to a well balanced riding program.

It has been a pleasant task for me to read this book written by a sincere, dedicated and perhaps most important —, an open-minded horsewoman.

Jimmy Williams

PREFACE

When it was suggested that I write this book, the need w
stressed for a manual for teachers of intermediate and advanc
Western riding. This book is designed to answer the need not on
of the teacher, but the beginner, advanced and intermediate rid
as well.

In accepting the assignment, I want to say, with due humilit
that this book and the principles and methods it sets forth have bee
derived from the many years I have spent watching, studying ar
learning from top riders and trainers of the Western horse, in tl
show ring, in the arena, and at work on the ranch.

People of the West have been accustomed to thinking of ridir
as something that just came naturally, with effort and practice, lil
walking or running. Only recently have we come to recognize tl
value of a study of riding.

Why should the Westerner study riding?

For the same reason we study and increase our skill in ar
physical activity.

The Western boy knows how to run, but if he wants to wi
the hundred yard dash for his school, he studies with the tra
coach and learns to run so as to get the greatest speed from his bod
with the least strain. The training the track coach gives him ha
been worked out from the experience of many people and fro
many years of study of the human physique and what it is capab
of and the best way to develop that capability.

The same is true of horsemanship, but here the challenge
double. Not one, but two living creatures, the horse and the ride
are involved. When they work smoothly together, a partnership ha
been achieved, a kind of unity which dates from before writt
history and which has done much to influence the history of tl
world. From time immemorial, the horseman has been a figure
romance, in ancient ballads and stories, even as he is one in today
television.

But, besides playing cops and robbers through the centurie
mounted men have won battles, carried vital messages, run thri
ing races, hunted stags, foxes and other animals, and forme
triumphal processions. In America, not only was the continent co
quered by the mounted Spanish, but horsemen explored the wilde
ness and made possible the great empire of the West.

True, the horse suffered a temporary loss of prestige with tl coming of the machine. Automobile, truck, and tractor have taken over some of his jobs.

But now, as we enter the space age, the horse is far from obsolete. His beauty, if nothing else, will always make him an object of man's cherishing. The excitement he provides on the race track and in the hunting field, not to mention the exercise and recreation he makes possible, keep him in the good graces of Easterner and Westerner alike.

The Western horse, however, has a greater value in the scheme of things because he has so many uses. Ranchmen are finding that mechanization on the range has its limits. No jeep can work cattle like an intelligent, well-trained horse. No machine can provide quite the thrill of the rodeo. With growing interest in riding for recreation as well as for a livelihood, young Westerners are going in for the show ring, the arena and for racing.

All this leads naturally to the need for training of both horses and riders.

A well-schooled horse, ridden by a well-schooled horseman, can not only surpass untrained rivals in show and rodeo, but can do better work at home on the ranch. The same horse, if he is good enough and is properly schooled and ridden, should be able to win as a barrel racer for Sis, come back and carry Mamma in a pleasure class, and then carry Daddy as a cutting horse. On the ranch, he can work cattle for Dad and round out his service for the whole family by accommodating four-year-old Bud in first riding lesson .

And, also important to an owner, who values his mount and, it is hoped, loves him, the horse, ridden properly and escaping the needless abuse of bad horsemanship, will have a longer span of life and usefulness.

It is with this principle in mind — enabling a rider to get the maximum of pleasure and usefulness from his horse with least strain on both horse and rider — that the system of teaching in this book has been worked out.

I do not say that this is the only way to learn and teach good riding. I only say that, through years of working with the horse observing and using almost every technique known to man in trying to perfect a horse's ability to handle himself and work under a rider, I have arrived at the methods given here. I hold riding clinics because I want people to enjoy their horses, and I school horses because I want them to work willingly for people. Where is there more grace and beauty than in the sight of a rider who enjoys his horse and a horse that will work for his rider?

Riding, since it has to do with living creatures, is a constantly developing skill, adapting to changing conditions. It is a never ending source of knowledge. There can be. no absolutely hard and fast rules. Never was there a truer saying than, "A horse will make a liar out of you, every time."

But if this book makes life easier for one horse, makes one person enjoy that horse more, or helps one devoted teacher put over correct horsemanship to a class, then I have made this book worthwhile.

It is with this in mind that I dedicate this book to that most exasperating, most fascinating and most admirable of animals — the *horse*.

SUZANNE NORTON JONES — BIOGRAPHY

"Born in the saddle," Suzanne Norton Jones, instead of the proverbial "silver spoon in her mouth," had the "feel" of horsemanship in her hands, from babyhood.

Before she could walk, she was taught to sit a horse. Her teacher was her father, Lt.-Col. A. H. Norton of the U.S. Cavalry. As she grew up, she saw and participated in some of the best riding this continent has ever produced.

Suzanne herself began winning cups and ribbons for horsemanship before she was six. At seven, competing with adults, including Olympic team riders of 1932 from Fort Bliss, the child won pole bending, stake racing and jumping awards at the 111th Cavalry Show in Las Vegas, N.M.

Her family background in New Mexico gave her a special interest in Western riding. Since the 1930's she has been showing in timed events all over the West, finding time to keep her horsemanship ready for top performance while she attended Mary Washington College in Virginia and, later, the University of Arizona.

In recent years, Suzanne Norton Jones was Rodeo Queen at California Polytech, San Luis Obispo, Calif.; Champion Cow Girl of the Intercollegiate Rodeo, Tucson; has competed and won in California, Arizona, New Mexico, Texas, Kansas and Colorado in barrel races, flag races, reining, stock horse, and other Western classes. Twice she has brought home the trophy for Champion Western Riding Horse from the New Mexico State Fair, and she holds a trophy for Champion Stock Horse at the American Royal, Kansas City. She has judged Western events and reining in shows in many states as far east as Florida, as far west and north as Washington State.

Mrs. Jones, drawing on her extensive background of knowledge and experience, has held many "Clinics" to help teachers correctly introduce Western riding. She is a member of the National Riding Committee of the Division of Girls and Women's Sports of the American Association for Health, Physical Education and Recreation, a department of the National Education Association, an organization which, with Perry-Mansfield Camps, has co-sponsored Western Clinics at Roswell, N.M., with Mrs. Jones as principal instructor.

She has also held clinics at Perry-Mansfield Camps in Steamboat Springs, Colo., followed by one-day clinics for 4-H Clubs of the vicinity; and for the Extension Division and Animal Husbandry Department of Colorado State University.

She is a recognized judge of 6 breeds including the quarter horse, Appaloosa, palomino and Arabian and is on the Board o Directors for Stock Saddle Seat of the the American Horse Show Association.

At home, Suzanne Norton Jones and her husband, R. C (Punch) Jones, cattle and sheep rancher of Tatum, N.M., raise and train quarter horses and thoroughbreds. Their staff of helpers includes their four children, Deborah, 11; Clayborne, 10; Dirk, 8 and Michelle, 5 — as well as 20-year-old "Dun Gone," the equine baby-sitter.

— end —

CONTENTS

PART I

BEGINNER

Chapter I

THE BEGINNER

Any one is potentially a rider. With this thought in mind the greatest of care should be taken in the introduction of a would-be rider to his horse. For only through the complete understanding of the horse and its ways can a human ever attempt to become a member of the "horseman" family. (Ill. 1, a, b, c, d)

The horse is essentially a timid, docile animal that flees from its enemies instead of fighting; he is easily startled by unfamilair objects, noises and quick movements — his life depends on flight and thousands of years of domestication has not removed this instinct.

Despite the comparative huge mass that is a horse, often looked on as an object of fear, they are very simple creatures. They have the mentality of about a three year old child; they respond to gentleness, respect authority, will rebel against cruelty. A tone of voice may send a horse to the back side of a corral, a quick movement may cause an even quicker kick, instinctive, protective.

Possibly the first thing to do with beginners is to let them watch horses not only in the stall, but in the pasture; let them observe the horse being schooled, let them watch older or more experienced riders around the horses. Explain to them what was well done or badly done as far as the horse's understanding is concerned; i.e., a rider whipped the horse maybe for kicking at another horse, as far as the beginner is concerned, they should understand that punishment of a horse should be instantaneous (before the horse's mind has slipped off onto something else), done quickly and not prolonged. The horse kicked, he should be spanked once, twice then no more. The punishment must be *just.* Prolonged punishment of any kind brings rebellion and from rebellion comes your outlaw — *man made,* few so very, very few are the "psychos" in the horse world that can not work for man.

(It seems I am invariably referring to a teacher, because there is generally some one else around to bring a beginner and introduce him to the horse world. But sometimes this is not the situation, the reader simply steps into the shoes of the teacher, and becomes the teacher of himself. A very difficult job, but a rewarding one — for there is no one that can teach to another if they are not receptive, so really the strictest diciplinarian and teacher is the person himself . . .)

The beginner should learn to handle a horse on the ground, groom him, feed him, care for his needs. This simple handling not only introduces the beginner to the ways of a horse but also helps him to gain confidence around a horse, to learn his needs, to under-stand his behavior pattern. A horse is a massive creature — but even a child of five — some 35 pounds — can control him and be safe around him.

A beginner should not only gain confidence around a horse but also have respect for what is possible for the horse to do — the hu-man is the thinking member of the horse-rider combination.

A few simple rules:

1. Never stand directly in front of a horse.
2. Don't stand directly behind a horse.
3. In leading, lead from the left side, your shoulder beside the horse's shoulder.
4. Do not loop the reins or rope around any part of your body, including your hand.
5. In picking up their feet, be careful about where your feet are, be parallel to your horse, and facing to the rear.
6. In moving around a horse, particularly around the hindquart-ers, be sure the horse has turned around and looked at you. Though they do not appear to be asleep, they may be, and to touch them will bring an instanteous kick or a violent shy-ing to one side.
7. Keep your hand flat in hand feeding, fingers feel like good carrots.
8. Don't have loose horses where horse's are tied.
9. Be sure all your equipment is in good state of repair, halter, rope, reins, bridle, cinch, cinch strap, etc.
10. Be careful, if your horse or someone else's horse is a stranger, a horse will instinctively strike or kick when a new horse comes up.

The 10 rules above, why are they necessary if a horse is gentle and well broken? No one can foresee when a car might back-fire behind a horse, or a cat and dog may come flying around the barn. It is wise to be prepared. You might blame the horse for step-ping on your toe, but is is really your fault for not paying attention to what your horse is doing and what is going on around you. These rules apply to doctoring also. You may know that you are helping the horse get well, but he doesn't. He will protect his head by strik-ing or biting, as he will protect the rest of his body by kicking, bit-ing, striking or fleeing.

After a beginner has a good knowledge of the horse, he can be-gin his riding by riding bareback. Why? A person that starts bare-back can acquire balance, feel, and confidence which cannot be learned with a saddle — he learns to ride by the "seat of his pants". Also, strangely enough, though it is easier to fall off bareback, it is safer, because there is no way for a rider to get "hung up."

While the rider is in a small corral he can play around on the horse slide off of him, turn around backward, etc. The fear of falling off is great in beginning riders, even when the dismount is called for by an instructor. It is good for the rider to learn to swing off and land on his feet. It is surprising how many horses will stop when they feel a rider begin to slide off and this sliding off helps the rider overcome the fear of the distance from horse to ground.

There are a few foolhardy people that have no conception of a horse's ability and limitation, but most people will progress and do what they feel they are capable of doing . . . When the beginner has played around on the still horse enough that he feels he is ready for movement, let him walk the horse out or let someone lead the horse around the pen. This movement is a fascinating thing so different than a bicycle or any other moving vehicle — here are two living creatures that must work together — the horse and the rider!

At the walk the rider learns to go with the movement of the horse to feel the movement of the horse; if bareback, the leg should hang relaxed from the knee down, the grip of the lower leg will not keep a rider on, but the balance and position of body from the knees up will.

After the beginner has walked around several times, he should learn how to control direction of the horse's movement, let him stop the horse by pulling back on the reins, squeeze the leg and lean slightly forward to make the horse go forward. It is important for the beginner to know the simple mechanics of controlling the horse: The reins or bit is the brake and the steering wheel, the legs are the accelerator; the weight can be used to aid the steering wheel, the brake and the accelerator depending on where it is used; the voice also helps the brake and the accelerator. These four aids: legs, hands (reins), weight and voice are the method of speaking to a horse. When a rider understands the four aids it is very easy for them to understand why a rider should ride certain ways in order to have a horse perform for them.

It is *not* absolutely imperative for a rider to begin bareback, but there is a certain amount of balance and poise that a bareback rider has that cannot be acquired any other way, there is a certain amount of feel of a horse that he acquires which cannot be acquired through the saddle. Too often a teacher that has done bareback riding in the past, forgot that they did ride bareback and that they still have the "feel" of a horse, (the balance so imperative in good riding) so he does not have his own pupils·do some bareback riding.

In young beginners often they progress faster with 30 minute lessons every day then with hour lessons twice a week. There is no better teacher than experience or "miles in the saddle".

When the beginner has learned to stop and start a horse and can control him to a degree, particularly for the stop, they may be taken to a larger area or allowed to go into a faster gait. It is wise for a beginner to start on a gentle, quiet, obedient and soft-gaited horse. Never over-mount a rider regardless of what phase of riding he is in. A particularly young or apprehensive rider can be led on foot or beside another horse until he has confidence in his ability to control not only himself but his horse.

A beginner should understand the why's and wherefor of a horse, he should have confidence in this ability to handle the horse on the ground and mounted.

Understanding
Confidence
Ability

These are beginner pre-requisites.

The bareback riding can be deserted now with the knowledge that even in the saddle almost every rule applies also to the bareback rider — with the main aim of bareback riding to develop confidence, feel and balance.

If the rider has enough confidence in himself when he starts on the saddle he will not instinctively grab the saddle horn. The saddle horn is really the bane of western riding. It is not the hand that can keep the rider from falling off, but the leg. With that very tempting saddle horn sitting just in reach even the reins are often thrown away when a beginner madly grabs for the horn. The main intention of the horn is not a hold, but to tie to for roping.

A beginning rider should be able to walk, jog, lope, halt, back. circle and half circle or reverse.

Sometimes in the transition from one gait to another ie. walk to jog or jog to lope it is necessary to ride behind the beginner (he has developed such a mental barrier against the next gait). The security of someone behind him with encircling arms often completely erases any fear he may have had, and his next step in progress is begun.

The position, which is given further in the text, should be explained to the rider so he has a complete understanding of why it should be thus. Why should the heels be down? To keep the ankle flexed, to elongate the calf muscles for better contact, to keep the heel from clutching the horse's sides.

Why not lean forward when you halt a horse? The aid to go forward is body inclination forward. Don't tell the horse to stop and go at the same time.

A nice exercise to help develop position and stability of leg is to stand in the stirrups — with the heels down, and ankle relaxed; this exercise can be done at whatever gait the rider is up to.

In all beginner work, after confidence has been established, the desire is not to shake that confidence but to keep developing it — slowly, carefully.

The beginner must have understanding of everything that is done on the ground and upon a horse; he must have confidence in himself, his mount and his teacher; he must develop the ability to do for himself and his mount what must be done.

Elementary basic control—stop, go, turn and position are hand and foot. Bring them along together. And with them bring the BE-GINNER!

In all of this introduction of the beginner to the horse do not overlook letting him play — on horseback; at first there can be walking tag, walking races, leading races. There are limitless games that can be done on horseback to relax the rider and let him enjoy his riding. As he progresses in ability the speed of the game can increase; cross country riding can be done with strict observance of good horsemanship rules.

Any one is potentially a rider, it is up to the person himself or to his teacher if he is to be able to seek or hold the reins of "horsemanship" and become a "horseman".

Camp Riding

Due to the circumstances in which summer camp riding has to be taught it was thought beneficial to have an insert added pertaining to this field.

Two situations exist for summer camps which makes the teaching of summer camp riders slightly different: Beginning riders completely unacquainted with livestock of any kind and leased horses completely unacquainted with children in any form!

In order to bring these two together the horses should come into the camp at least two weeks before it commences so that they may be handled and ridden by the teachers or assistants. The normal camp routine should be followed as near as possible with the horses working on a loose rein at all gaits, in other words well-balanced or "stabilized". With no horse-manner problems a teacher can progress rapidly. Due to the short time horse and rider are together, and the horses and riders being what they are, it is not **advisable** to work campers bareback—bareback riding may be offered later as a reward "plum" for the more advanced riders.

As the horses have been acquainted with proper conduct, so should the children be properly introduced to the rules governing their conduct around and on their horses. An assistant, if there are enough, may be assigned to each rider. These assistants will supervise the mounting, dismounting, checking of equipment, etc. Depending on camp procedures they may walk beside the beginner, or mounted may lead the beginner beside them. Until the child has lost all fear and can concentrate on himself and his position the assistant should remain beside him.

The working area should be small and the classes divided into small groups of as near equal ability as possible. A small enclosed ring is of great importance to the mental quietness of both horse and rider.

The "standing" position is important in this phase of teaching, not only for balance, but muscular coordination. First taught at a halt the young camper can begin to learn to get the feel of position—heels down, flexed ankle, etc.—they begin to feel a oneness with the horse.

After a short lesson in this, they may be led at the walk by their assistant, when confident and able they should be asked to stand in their stirrups at the slow trot or jog. Working this way it is quite easy for a young rider to develop security of seat so important in effective control. At any gait the rider may put his free hand either on the middle of the horse's neck or on the swells of the saddle to get the feel of motion without abusing the horse either by jerking on the mouth with an unsteady hand or falling back into the saddle and bouncing on his loins.

Due to the leverage action of the curb and if the horses are use to it, the snaffle bit is found to be practical for some campers. The use of two hands also keeps both hands of the young rider occupied and helps in his maintenance of balance and control.

The first five lessons deal mostly with rider balance, fundamentals of position and balance, and elementary control — where the brake, steering wheel and accelerator are.

The posting trot may be taught at this period, as the "standing" position, the mechanics should first be taught at the halt. The instructor may ask for standing position, then "sit" or say "up" and "down". From the halt the young rider goes to the walk and then to the slow trot. Do not overtax the young riders physically and mentally—take a break when necessary, keep them seeking more knowledge and more skill.

Handled with care and caution the young camper that has never touched a horse; and the horse that has never had the caress of a child can give to each other an introduction to a new, life and a life time of happiness in a horseman's world.

Ill. 1

Ill. 1a
Anyone is Potentially a Rider

19

Ill. 1b
From Confidence

Ill. 1c
Comes Competence

In the Corral—at 4

In the Show Ring—at 8

In the Arena—at 10
Ill. 1d

22

COMMON HORSE FACTS
Breeds Of Western Horse

Almost all light horse breeds of horses are used or can be used under the western saddle, which type depends on what job is to be done.

The American Saddle horse is used generally in the show ring in western pleasure American Saddle horse classes or on the bridle path as a pleasure horse.

The Appaloosa though once used as a war horse and originally in the United States an Indian horse, this breed is now used as a stock horse, pleasure or parade horse. Some breeders use them to do ranch work. The Appaloosa is a very colorful and adaptable individual.

The Arabian, the oldest of the light horse breeds, was primarily developed as a saddle horse. A comparatively small horse, individuals range from 14.0-15.1 hands. This breed is used on the range and in the show ring, as a pleasure horse, stock horse.

The Morgan, the "first family of American horses", is an all around utility horse — his work ranging from light draft to pleasure work.

The Palomino, the golden horse of history, has developed to a type in the southwest which is almost synonymous with the quarter horse. Some of the most outstanding show horses of the quarter breed are double registered as quarter horses and palominos. Especially a western horse, they have also been used as parade horses, bridle path or pleasure horses due to their outstanding color.

The Pinto, descendants of the Spanish horses, is divided primarily into two groups, the western horse and the parade type. As in the Appaloosa and Palomino, the Pinto's desirability stems from personal color preference.

The Quarter Horse, essentially a horse of the West, is a breed derived for racing a quarter of a mile back in the early Virginia days. Today this breed dominates the arena, the western show ring, the ranches, the pleasure trails, and the race track. The quarter horse is encroaching upon the thorobred in the jumping ring and on the polo field — the thorobred, quarter horse cross is one of the most popular crosses for a do-it-all, all around individual.

The Tennessee Walking Horse, the Plantation Walking Horse, is sometimes used, due to its comfortable gaits as a pleasure horse.

The Thorobred, orginally bred for and as a race horse; this breed has developed into an almost all purpose horse as a riding horse. As a race horse it has no equal, the thorobred or the thorobred cross excels on the quarter race track, in the show ring, the arena, on the polo field, in the hunt field and on the ranch. The most adaptable of all riding horses seems to be the thorobred-quarter horse cross.

Clothes For A Rider

1. Hat
2. Shirt
3. Belt
4. Blue jeans or Levis
5. Boots
6. Gloves (opt.)
7. Chaps (opt.)

Grooming Equipment

1. Body Brush
2. Dandy Brush
3. Curry Comb
4. Hoof Pick
5. Mane Comb
6. Mane and tail comb
7. Body Sponge
8. Scraper
9. Rub Rag
10. Shedding Blade

Bridle — (ILL. 2)

1. Nose Band
2. Brow Band.
3. One Ear Crown Piece
4. Cheek Piece
5. Throat Latch
6. Bit
7. Lip Strap (opt.)
8. Reins
9. Curb strap or Chain

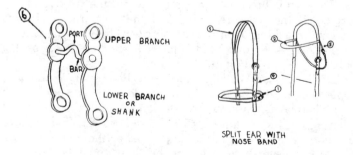

ILL. 2 PARTS OF BIT AND BRIDLE

Hackamore — (Ill. 3)

1. Brow Band
2. Bosal
3. Fiador Knot
4. Mecate Reins

Saddle — (Ill. 3)

1. Horn
2. Swells
3. Pommel Binding
4. Seat
5. Cantle
6. Concho
7. Rear Housing (Back Jockey)
8. Skirt
9. Rigging
10. Dee Ring
11. Saddle Strings
12. Flank Billet
13. Flank Cinch
14. Connecting Cinch Strap
15. Cinch
16. Stirrup
17. Fender
18. Latigo Strap
19. Rigging D. Ring
20. Rigging
21. Latigo Carrier
22. Front Jockey
23. Skirt
24. Throat

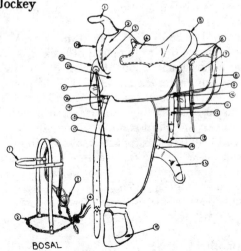

BOSAL

ILL. 3 PARTS OF SADDLE AND HACKAMORE

25

Rules Of Good Horsemanship

1. Move and talk quietly around a horse.
2. Groom properly before and after riding, clean feet both times.
3. If necessary keep horse properly shod, at a month to six week interval between shoeing.
4. Have their teeth checked at regular intervals.
5. Worm every three months.
6. Keep bot fly eggs cleaned off legs and body.
7. Feed horse regularly, at a minimum of twice a day.
8. Be sure horse has access to water.
9. Give tetanus, sleeping sickness and distemper vaccine at regular intervals.
10. Upon leaving the barn walk a half a mile or warm up 15 minutes before increasing the gait. Return the same way.
11. Be as courteous on horseback as you are expected to be on the ground.
    a. Don't rush by another horse,
    b. Don't cut directly in front of them,
    c. Stay off another horse's heels. Remember a strange horse is invariably considered an enemy.
    d. On the track to the right or on fence stay outside, or on the fence.
    e. On the track to the left stay on the inside.
12. Keep your equipment, horse and yourself clean and neat.

Common Blemishes Or Unsoundness

Bone Spavin — bony enlargement of the hock

Bog spavin — an inflammation or swelling at the hock, comparable to sprained ankle.

Capped elbow, shoe boil — swelling at the point of elbow.

Capped hock — swelling at the point of hock.

Curb — an enlargement about three inches below point of hock.

Ring bone — bony enlargement involving the pasterns.

Side bone — ossification of the lateral cartilage.

Splint — exostoses along the cannon which may be caused by a blow or a break of the splint bone.

Stinghalt — a peculiar jerking action of the hind leg.

Thoroughpin — a soft enlargement forward of the point of hock generally connected with the bog spavin.

Bowed tendon — thickening of the suspensory ligament or flexor tendon generally due to strain.

Windpuff — distention of the synovial bursae in the fetlock joint area.

Any or all of these may cause an unsoundness, they may be only a blemish acquired, or inherited, or they may be an unsoundness, acquired or inherited.

Medicines — First Aid

It is often wise to keep a small supply of medicines on hand for the time a veterinarian is not immediately available or if of minor consequence and does not require a vet.

1. Clean sterile gauze: roll and pads
2. An elastic adhesive tape
3. Thermometer
4. Epsom salts
5. An antibiotic ointment
6. Iodine—7%
7. Mineral oil
8. Vaseline or wool fat
9. Disinfectant
10. Poultice powder
11. Alcohol
12. Disposable syringes & needles
13. Colic medicine, prescribed by your veterinarian
14. Eye ointment, prescribed by your veterinarian
15. Hoof dressing

Glossary Of Terms

Aids — means of communication to a horse (legs, hands, weight, voice).

Block — a bale of hay can be roughly divided into 5-6 blocks, an average feeding.

Chip — about half a block of hay.

Calf knee — knees bend backwards.

Cow hock — hocks turn in toward each other.

Colt — male horse under five years.

Cold-blood — an animal of no breeding.

Ewe neck — from the withers to the poll the neck is concave, as in the ewe.

Favor — a slight limp.

Filly — female horse under five years.

Foal — male or female young horse under one year.

Green — a horse that has been broken, but has had little schooling.

Hackamore — a "bridle" that contains no mouthpiece.

Half-bred — generally half thorobred, the rest may be unknown.

Hand — four inches, used to measure a horse.

Mare — female horse.

Mutton wither — the withers are low and not clearly defined as in the sheep.

Near side — left side of the horse.

Off side — right side of horse.

Parrot mouth — upper teeth protrude in front of the lower teeth.

Pig eye — small eyes

Pony — a horse under 14.2 hands.

Smooth mouth — a horse over 10, aged.

Stallion — a male horse.

Star gazer — a horse that holds his head and nose high.

Tack — riding equipment.

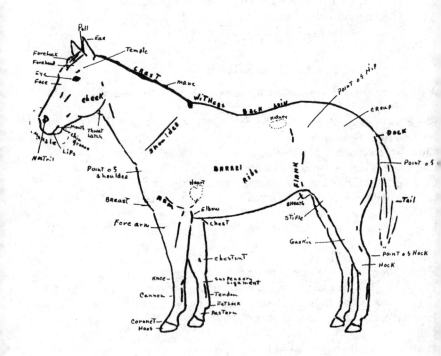

ILL. 3a PARTS OF HORSE

PART II

INTERMEDIATE

Chapter I

TEACHER AND CLASS

The first meeting of teacher and class is always a two-way evaluation period. Class takes teacher's measure, as far as they are able on a first contact. Teacher sizes up pupils as accurately as can be done.

The teacher of Western riding sometimes has it a little harder than instructors in other fields because often he is an experienced rider but has never been a teacher.

However, let us say that you, our teacher, experienced or not, stand in the teaching arena, with a group of young riders before you. For the purposes of this part of the book, they are not beginners. They not only have "ridden all their lives," they at least claim to have learned the rudiments of good horsemanship.

That is, having finished beginner's training, they are able to:

Walk
Jog
Lope
Halt
Back
Circle
Half-circle or reverse

They have fairly decent seat and position.

They are able to do limbering-up exercises (see Chap. V) at a walk and at a jog.

You will discover much of how valid their claims are in this first lesson.

Goal of both students and instructor is to increase the skill and dexterity of these riders until they are ready for advanced schooling and patterns.

Well, you, the teacher, must start somewhere. At the beginning is as good a place as any.

The beginning is the establishment of good working relations with the pupils.

Ask the class to line up, in a straight line, facing you, with ample interval between horses as a safety factor. Introduce yourself and tell them what name they may call you. "I am Bob McConnell. Call me Mr. McConnell." Let them introduce themselves and tell you the name of their horses.

Since you and the class are new to each other, the next thing is to explain some of the terminology you plan to use.

Also, since you are in a phase of some importance here, you

have considered your voice beforehand. If you have a strong, clear voice, well and good. If not, you have brought along a megaphone or arranged for a public speaking system. In any case, watch your enunciation. It is important that the class understand you.

When you have finished speaking, the class should know that "track" means the path just inside the arena fence (or some other designated area).

"Track to right" means the rider should turn so that his right hand is toward the center of the arena. "Track to left" indicates that left hand should be toward the center of the arena.

To "circle right" the riders describe a complete circle, tangent to the track, and retake the track at the point where they left it. Size of the circle depends on speed of gait. At a walk, make circle 2 yards in diameter; at jog, 4 yards; at lope, 6 yards.

When "half-circle right" or "reverse" is called, the riders leave track as if for full circle right, but half way around return obliquely to the track on the left hand.

"Half-turn in reverse" consists of an oblique, followed by a half-circle.

You, or some other advanced rider, demonstrate each movement.

If the class is unfamiliar with the terms, it is unlikely that they will retain them clearly in memory after the lesson. Therefore, at the conclusion of the class, it is advisable to hand out diagrams like Ill. 4. Copies of this diagram have been run off on a mimeograph or ditto machine.

Having given the class a little challenge with terminology, go very briefly over the principles of position — i.e., heels down, ankles relaxed; leg contacting horse at inside upper calf, knee and thigh; seat in middle of saddle; arms at side, elbows slightly in front of body, or brushing body; rein arm bent at elbow, position in front of or above saddle horn depending on horse's head position; head and eyes up, shoulders back and down, chest up, "tall in the saddle."

The class has now been still long enough. Rail work is coming up. But first caution the students on distance between horses and emphasize the need to pass on the inside. Give reasons. Let a rider demonstrate.

Now send the class to the rail for work and to enable you to make your first evaluations of each rider and horse and their problems for straight rail work.

Watch position, gauge degree of skill and probable bitting problems or horse trouble. Note general level of class and determine whether some riders need extra work.

Work the class at walk, jog, lope, both ways of the ring.

Ask them to ride in, facing you. Go over position, in more detail this time.

Now the horses are standing still. While they are at halt, tell the students why heels should be down, ankles flexed and relaxed, stirrup at the broad (ball) part of the foot.

Explain that the degree the foot should be turned out depends greatly· on the conformation of the rider, but it generally should not exceed 30°.

You can illustrate this by taking as examples the tallest rider in the class and one of medium size, if such riders can be chosen without embarrassing them because of calling attention to very long or very short legs. Conformation of the horse's barrel is a factor, too. Point this out.

Select a pupil whose position illustrates that the weight of the foot on the stirrup should be slightly toward the big toe, or flat, not towards the little toe.

Explain the importance of having upper calf, knee and thigh in contact with the horse. (This contributes to a secure seat).

When the seat is at the middle of the saddle, there should be a three-point contact, the two seat bones and the crotch making a deep seat.

Position of arms and use of reins can be reviewed and emphasized with demonstrations. Upper body should be erect, without stiffness.

By this time, if you look at your watch, lesson time will probably be over.

Dismiss the class, always with a word of encouragement and a brief sentence or two about the next lesson or lessons. Always keep your class looking forward to challenge and achievement.

So . . . . The first session is over.

You start home, perhaps with your own horse in a trailer behind your car.

You have seen your class actually ride. Let us say that, as you drive home, you decide, on sober reflection, that, with one or two exceptions calling for special attention, your group is well prepared for intermediate work.

Now that you are assured of this, your teaching plans can be definite and you are justified in setting them an interesting and relatively demanding course.

However, before the next lesson, you would do well to meditate on four steps of teaching that have been found to apply to instruction in any field of physical activity.

These are: Demonstration. Execution by students. Evaluation. Repetition.

Try to utilize this system consistently. Toss it around, try it.

It can be applied to any phase, any time and any level of teaching

For instance, as you drive along, you might visualize applying this method to teaching the stop.

1. Demonstration and Explanation.

    a. Show a good, well-balanced stop at speed.

    b. Explain the aids used, the correct behavior of the horse in answering these aids, and the steps to obtaining the stop.

2. Execution by Students.

    a. Let the class go to the rail and stop from the walk on command. When they are ready (and this may not be for two weeks or more), work them at jog, then at lope.

3. Evaluation.

    a. Call them all back in quickly, evaluate their performance; briefly go over procedure; send them back, either individually or as a class, to the rail.

4. Repetition.

    a. Work the stop. Call individuals in if their problems are individual. Repetition is as important to the rider as to the horse.

    b. Give suggestions to class as a whole to help correct faults. It is always better to praise pupils' good points, even if you have to pick them out of the air, than to give criticism and too many suggestions for improvement.

As you approach home and look forward to rest for both you and your horse, devote a final period of meditation to three components of a very effective over-all teaching method: the introductory lesson to evaluate and establish contact; the "four-point" system of demonstration, execution by students, evaluation and repetition; ability on the teacher's part to instruct clearly and always to answer the pupils' request to know "why."

Never forget to give your pupils the "why," even if they should not ask for it. It is fine to say, "Use the leg at the cinch," but you should also give the "why" — which is "to move the horse's forehand."

Let your riders fully understand the why's and wherefore's.

Nothing is more gratifying than to have your own alert and well-informed pupil beat you in a reining class.

When you can make someone better than you are yourself — you are a teacher!

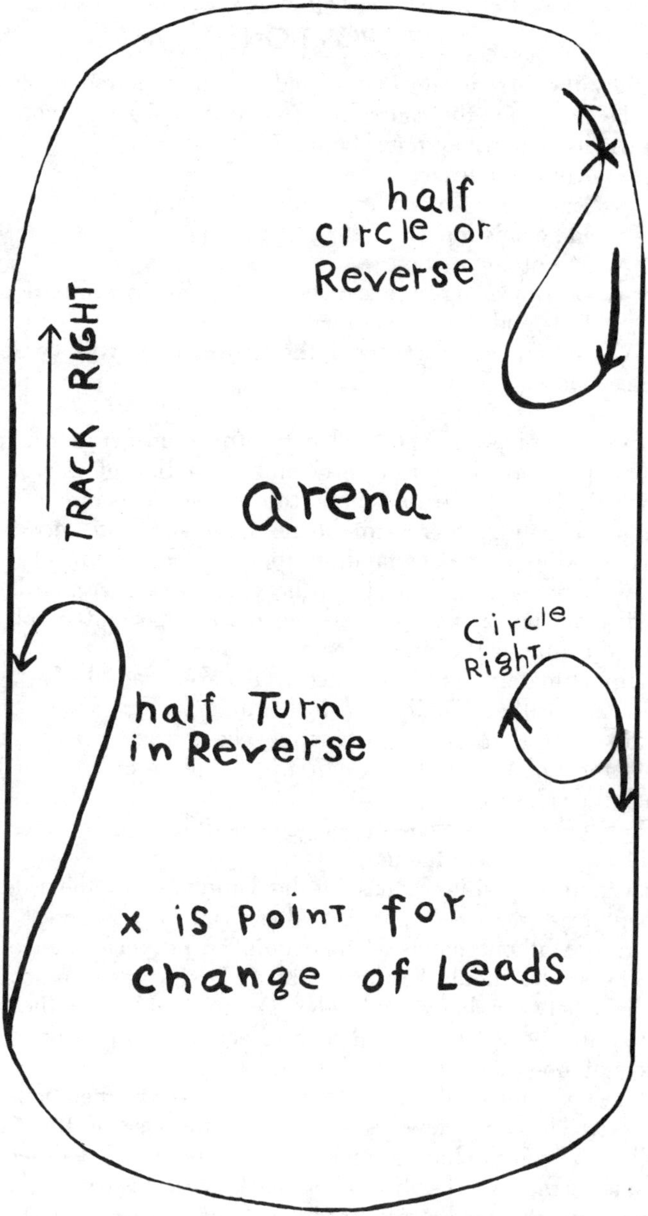

half
circle or
Reverse

TRACK RIGHT

arena

Circle
Right

half Turn
in Reverse

x is point for
change of Leads

Ill. 4

POSITION

Now the first lesson is past and you have found your students all to be ready for the course of intermediate training you plan for them. At its conclusion, they should:

Know the leads;

Know the use and application of aids;

they should be able to:

Maintain position;

Do limbering-up exercises at all gaits, including lope;

Ride and show a schooled horse.

When they have mastered the above, they will be ready for advanced riding.

* * * *

In developing an expert rider, the first consideration is position. Without position, there can be no understanding of aids or control. Without aids and control, there can be no schooling of a horse. Without schooling, there can be no understanding between horse and rider. With no understanding, there will be no unity. And from oneness of horse and rider stems the good working ranch horse, the valued show horse, and — perhaps most important of all for the future of riding — the child's horse.

Unfortunately, or fortunately (I never can decide which, I myself am rather flexible with a student-rider about details of individual position, there just cannot be a rigid measuring stick, for instance, as to how long a stirrup should be or how far forward or back the rider's leg.

Let us take the elements of good position one by one, first for the rider on a horse at the halt:

Certainly, position starts at the bottom, with the rider's legs. Without legs in correct position, there can be no correct seat and no hands. Without hands, there would be no performance.

The ankles should be flexed, thus allowing them to act as shock absorbers between horse and rider. A stiff ankle jars the rider all the way up the spine. This in turn affects the horse, due to the discomfort of a bouncing rider on his back.

Heels should be down, helping the ankles in their job as shock absorbers. The heel down stretches the muscles of the calf, thus enabling the rider to have a clinging action with his lower leg. (Note: The side of the rider's calf, not the back or fleshy part, should be in contact with the saddle and ready to "talk" to the horse). Illus. 5.

Thus, the teacher should recommend a position of toe suited to a particular horse and rider but not greater than at an angle of 30° to the horse. A greater angle brings the knee out, resulting in loss of security and less leg contact.

Ill. 5

This front shot shows the rider's leg in light contact with the horse, again leaving the barrel of the horse where the curve of his barrel and the straight line of the rider's leg (calf) can no longer be together. On a deeper or longer barreled horse or a larger horse, this rider's legs could contact the horse's sides as far down as the ankle.

Ill. 5a

This close-up of the leg shows contact from the crotch down to where the straight bone of the calf of the rider's leg leaves the normal curve of the horse's barrel. The heel is down, the foot in a natural position, tending to be more parallel with, than at right angles to, the horse.

As for the foot, the broad part or ball of the foot is placed on the stirrup tread. This will vary slightly according to the type of stirrup used. If a broad or roping stirrup is used, the foot should give the appearance of being completely home, i.e., stirrup at heel. The ball of the foot is more or less the fulcrum of the rider's body with the majority of weight going out the heels. The weight in the stirrup should be only sufficient to maintain the stirrup. Another disadvantage of a stiff ankle is that it causes a rider to have too high a heel and to lose his stirrup.

The calf of the rider's leg has a clinging action to the horse. A well-schooled horse can and will obey leg aids given only by the calf. The leg follows the natural contour of the horse, leaving the horse's barrel at its widest part. (Illus. 5a) Never should the position of the leg be such that *from the knee down* the leg is going away from the horse. (Illus. 6) This is a common fault in certain areas where riders of saddle horses and walking horses have "gone Western."

Ill. 6
Unfortunately, the above position of the rider's feet is too often found with the leg leaving the horse at the knee in a very stiff and awkward angle instead of lying close to the horse's sides. The rider's toes are turned out too much. However, she is sitting nice and erect in the saddle.

The knee rests lightly against the saddle. It is as important for the knee to have flexion as the ankle. The more the horse is in motion, the greater the play in the rider's knee.

The rider's thighs cling to the saddle. The heavy part of the thighs should be in the rear of the thigh bones. This heavy part of the thigh has no part in riding. A person with extremely heavy thighs can help the situation by taking hold of his jeans and rolling the leg in toward the horse. This pulls the heavy muscles away from the saddle.

With hip joint relaxed and mobile, the rider should be able to bring his upper body forward or backward without displacing his seat or lower leg. The relaxed hip joint allows the rider to be in balance with his horse.

The rider's seat rests in the middle of the saddle, with the rider deep in the saddle on a three-point contact (the two seat bones and the crotch). Seated thus, the rider can be in position for any movement of the horse. If the rider inclines his torso back so that his seat bones are behind the movement of the horse, he will be "behind his horse" and fighting for his balance to keep up with the horse. Another common fault is "tucked hips," when the rider sits on his buttocks. This leads to cramped loin and bad leg control.

The upper body should be erect from point of hip to shoulder, with possibly a slight arch in the loin. The chest is lifted and shoulders held evenly. Due to the use of one hand on the reins in Western riding, it is important for a teacher to watch for the tendency of students to ride with the rein-hand-shoulder ahead of the other shoulder.

The arm is relaxed and moves independently of the body, with the elbow falling naturally, either slightly in front of the body or just brushing the body. The freedom of the arm from the body is essential so that it can convey the correct aids smoothly and quietly to the horse. Nervous and unsympathetic hands result in a nervous horse, a horse that tends to anticipate in order to avoid the harsh hand.

The wrist is light and relaxed and should not be cocked or knuckled-over. The hand should be a straight-line continuation of the arm.

The fingers, so all-important, must be relaxed, soft and pliable. The hands of the rider, remember, are the key to the horse's mouth. Regardless of how good a rider's seat and position may be, with no hands there can be no response from the horse's mouth. If hands were eliminated and communication limited to legs, weight and voice, then at least one-third of the control of the horse would be gone.

The rider's neck is erect, with head, chin and eyes up. The eyes should be up to allow the rider to see where he is going. For a rider to watch his horse is unnecessary and unsightly. The good rider is able to "feel" his horse.

Position of the rider's head is important. The human head is supported by a very slender shaft (the neck) and, in proportion to the rest of the body, is very heavy. Position of the rider's head will influence his whole body: lowered head often leads to round shoulders and humped back, and these in turn impair balance and security. To say "tall in the saddle" is to say "ride Western."

Ill. 7

This rider is riding a slightly short stirrup, as shown by the high knee. She could have her toe in a little more, a more relaxed ankle. Hip and upper body position are good.

Ill. 7a

Position here is quiet and relaxed. But the rider's leg should be further back. If she were to go into motion with this seat, she would be behind the action of her horse.

Ill. 8

Good, except that the rider's left shoulder is ahead of her right. Horse is jawing out and she is using too much rein. On the whole, however, she gives a quiet and workmanlike appearance.

Ill. 8a

Here the rider, riding with a short shank curb and with two hands, is obviously schooling; otherwise, the hands should have been up and above the saddle horn. Her toe should be in slightly, back of her calf, away from the horse. In motion, she shows that she gets her body with her horse.

Ill. 8b

This rider makes a pleasant picture. Her position is good, although her hand might preferably be above the saddle horn instead of in front of and below the horn.

Ill. 8c

The rider's hand should be down; toe should be in. Otherwise, this position is good.

Ill. 8d

Good. Note that an imaginary vertical line could be drawn from the rider's ear to her heel. The foot is compatible and she is nicely seated on three-point or crotch contact in the saddle.

The positions given above are for a rider not in motion. (Ill. 7, 7a)

In motion, the leg position, except when leg aids are applied, should remain the same. The seat should stay in the saddle, that is, the buttocks leave the saddle at speed but the crotch never leaves the saddle excessively. As speed increases, the rider's weight moves slightly forward, the weight being shifted down mostly to the thighs, knees, stirrups and heels.

In a change of gait to speed, the upper body should not fall behind the center of gravity of horse and rider, nor should it get in the rear of the base of support, which is the rider's legs. The inclination of the body will be forward *from the hip joints. Keep the seat and leg position quiet.* (Illus. 8, a, b, c, d)..

The rider must always be in balance with his horse. If you have the slightest doubt of this, try riding a trained reining horse without saddle or bridle. Even to stay on, you must be in balance.

In this chapter "position" has been taken element by element. Each part is vital. If one part is awry, then the whole position is imperfect.

The rider whose position is correct is graceful; he is relaxed without being sloppy; he looks workmanlike, not work-worn. Correct position is comfortable and unstrained for the rider and equally so for the horse, a position in which the rider can get a job of work done with maximum efficiency and at the same time present a picture of oneness with his horse. Beauty, grace and work all go together in this oneness.

Chapter III

AIDS

Teaching a pupil to ride falls into a natural sequence: Position, Aids, Movements.

A pupil cannot use the aids until he knows how to sit the horse properly. Until he knows the correct use of aids, he cannot control his horse in the various movements.

Aids may be defined as the code of communication from the rider to the horse. Since human beings have been unable to learn the language of the horse and no horse will ever get a Ph. D. in English, there must be other methods of communication between man and horse. These are the "aids."

The goal to seek in the application of the aids is for the horse to obey all you ask and the observer to see nothing of the application

The aids fall under four major headings — Legs, Hands, Weight and Voice.

It is through these four means, used individually or collectively or even in opposition to each other, that a horse is taught to respond. By repeated use of proper aids, a horse can respond to his rider's every whim.

In all work with horses, including use of the four aids, it should not be forgotton that their intelligence is generally on a par with that of a three-year-old child. Their power of retention is almost nil. Therefore, our relations with the horse are based on four essentials: Reward, Punishment, Patience, and the Forming of Habits.

To take the first three, every action directed by a rider toward a horse can be classified as "reward" or "punishment." To pull on the halter is punishment; to have no pull when the horse works beside you is "reward." To pull on the reins is "punishment," to release is "reward." To kick is "punishment," not to kick is "reward."

As for patience, when the rider stops to realize how many thousand of times he subjects the horse to varying degrees of reward and punishment in the hours he is mounted, patience on the rider's part seem entirely reasonable and there will be understanding of *why* a horse does what he does *when* he does it. Among a horse's faculties, patience is not one. It is therefore the rider's patience that leads to "reward."

Use of the first three essentials, Reward, Punishment and Patience, makes possible the fourth — the forming of Habits. Horses learn from habit, Good or bad, these habits can originate from only *one* source — the rider, or handler.

Bearing the four essentials in mind, we take up the aids.

First, Legs.

The legs of the rider are the wall between which the horse moves. They are used to urge the horse; to resist him; to yield. The legs have also been compared to the rudders of a ship — they are used to correct direction, to bring the horse's body "back on course."

The horse can be roughly divided into three parts — neck; shoulder and middle; and hindquarters. (Of course, there is an overlapping of all these parts). It is important to let the rider's legs control the parts of the horse's body which belong to leg-control and not use rein or hand aid too much.

There are two general leg positions, which for the sake of clarity, one may refer to as:

No. 1, at the cinch

No. 2, behind the cinch.

At the cinch (No. 1 position) is where the leg falls naturally. This is the position for control of the horse's shoulder and forehand and also may be the origin for impulsion or "go," which comes from the hindquarters. Control of the horse's shoulder and forehand will in time lead to ability to execute the rollback, pivot, spin and side pass. (The last is not a reining movement. It is used more for opening and closing gates and for positioning of a horse).

The rider's leg in No. 2 position, that is, about four inches behind the cinch, controls the horse's hindquarters. This position is generally used as a corrective one, i.e., when the horse has swung his hindquarters too much to one side, or the rider wishes to displace the hindquarters for control of the horse's body for a specified movement.

There are many different combinations in the application of the leg aids. For instance:

a. Left and right legs together at the cinch start movement straight forward or back and drive the horse into the bit.

b. Left leg at No. 1 and right leg at No. 2 will bend the horse around rider's left leg.

c. Left and right legs at No. 2 may hold the hindquarters from going to one side or the other while the horse is backing.

d. Right leg at No. 1, left leg at No. 2, will bend horse around the rider's right leg.

A well-schooled horse can and will obey a slight calf pressure, imperceptible to the observer. The rider applies calf pressure; if this is not obeyed, he uses heel pressure; if this is not obeyed, then the spur; if obedience is still not obtained, he may have to rely on the whip. But the application of the last two must be, oh, so tactful. The rider's legs, applied with skill and sensitivity, are as important to the horse's sides as are the hands, with their greater sensitivity, to the horse's mouth.

The legs at the horse's sides should be quiet and steady. Like the arms, they should be able to convey their meaning without interfering with, and without interference from, other parts of the body, such as the upper body or arms.

All leg movement should be smooth and tactful, only as energetic as the occasion demands.

The loose, swinging leg of his rider conveys utter confusion to a schooled horse. The loose leg may say "go," "turn," "faster," at the same time that the reins, or hand, are saying "slow down."

Too active or demanding a leg, on the other hand, will develop a horse that will try to *anticipate* in order to avoid *punishment*.

No horse objects to the aids if he understands them, and there is nothing more satisfying than to have horse and rider work together, not as leader and follower but as a pair, as graceful and fluent as dance partners.

The spur need only be used to reenforce the action of the calf or heel if a horse is slow in responding. Never allow a rider to wear a spur until he has enough seat and leg to use the spur properly. The spur should be used as an extension of the heel and must not be carried away from the horse's side and allowed to "bang" him when the rider desires action. The spurs, rightly used, "talk" as discreetly and quietly as a person murmuring secrets on a rural party line.

The whip, though carried in the rider's hand, is an extension of the leg aid. It may be used to punish, to enforce the leg aid, or to demand impulsion.

A rider with loose, swinging legs, regardless of the perfection of his balance, is leaving the horse only one line of communication and that is the hands. Why make the "language" barrier between horse and rider still higher by neglecting the leg aid?

Now as to weight. The use of weight as an aid refers to the minute shifting of the weight of the rider's hips. It does not refer to the shifting of weight of the upper body. This exaggerated side movement of the upper body and shoulders, which is so often inflicted on a horse working at speed, is a hinderance to the ability of the horse to work. Not only must he execute the movement required by the rider but he must, in some way, handle the 150 or more pounds that oppose his maneuverability.

The proper application of this aid is a slight weight shift forward from the hip joint to all movements which go forward. Shift of weight, forward or backward, is only such as to keep the rider in balance with the horse. Too often a rider has the misconception that he, with his 150 pounds more or less, can make the horse, with his 1,000 pounds or more, stop, go and turn, merely by exaggerated weight displacement.

When the weight aid is rightly used, the hips remain in the saddle; the weight displacement can be *felt* by the horse when the rider merely shifts from one seat bone to the other. This varying shift can be in any direction, forward, clockwise, counter-clockwise, or to the rear.

The horse, from the time he is first mounted, must learn to adjust his natural movements to the weight of man. The horse thus has made his concession. Now let the rider make his — not to interfere with the horse's ability to work and maneuver. Let the rider always place himself in balance and in position to be with the horse's movement if he expects the horse to work correctly and with maximum efficiency.

Note the change of position of the racing jockey, brought about by the successes early in the century of Tod Sloan, who rode crouched forward over his horse's withers, thus adjusting the weight of his body to the horse's center of gravity. Also note the change to the "balanced seat" of the rider of the jumping horse.

The western horse should not be forced to work under obsolete conceptions of weight and balance. Teach your students to get with their horses, to be with the movement.

The voice aid, though really not a "working" communication, is essential in the schooling of a horse. The effect of the voice, in speaking softly or in scolding, is all-powerful. Man cannot readily injure the hearing ability of a horse — and the equine ear is sensitive, so that almost any horse, even a badly trained one, is alert to a voice. Physical punishment often leads to rebellion, whereas one sharp scolding can do more good than ten whippings. As for praise and the soothing tone of your voice, a horse will seek these as readily as a child.

Remember, however, that the novice has a tendency to overdo the use of the voice aid.

And now we come to the most sensitive and vital aid of all. Hands. The rider's hands on the reins.

After the legs of the rider have put the horse into motion, the hands must control and direct this motion. Too much emphasis and study cannot be put on this phase of horsemanship.

The rein aids are four: No. 1, the direct rein; Nos. 2 and 3, the neck or bearing rein; No. 4, the leading rein.

Let us first mention that, due to the type of bit generally used on the Western horse, the curb bit, there is a limit to workability. It is very difficult to use a leading rein with this bit, since not only is there no direct pull on the horse's mouth, but also the leverage attained by the curb shank comes into effect, making the horse flex, which is not always desired. We will discuss bits and bitting at length in a later chapter.

No. 1, the direct rein, is the one most frequently used. Its function is to slow the horse down, to halt, back, and, in advanced schooling, it is used in coordination with the leg to put the horse into the bit. Its direction is straight rear.

Nos. 2 and 3, the bearing or neck rein, is used to turn a horse from a straight line to a curve. (For clarity, #3 rein is used when there is a rein action that asks the horse to shift his weight to the hindquarters). Its application should be as close to the horse's withers as the saddle horn will permit. In applying this rein, the hand should not move over four inches from the center of the horn to one side or the other. There is no need to carry the rein hand two feet or more to the side of the horse's neck to turn him. For a rollback to the right, No. 3 bearing rein carries an imaginary flight from the horse's mouth to the point of his inside hip. For rollback to the left, the left rein's flight is to the point of the horse's left inside hip.

No. 4 rein aid is the leading rein. Its application, as its name implies, is to lead. It is especially for use with young horses or in the re-schooling of horses that are put on the snaffle or hackamore.

The importance of the hands cannot be stressed too strongly. (Illus. 9, 9a)

Why? Because at the other end of the reins is the horse's mouth, that indispensable means of communication. Give me the best of riders, the strongest of riders — if he has no hands, I want him not. He is not a horseman. He is only a rider. His horses? Just machines, with no feeling, no soul. These priceless qualities have been torn from them — by his hands. Such a rider has no "feel." And without feeling, how can there be harmony, beauty, the *simpatico*, as the Spanish say, the oneness that is sought by the horseman?

Watch a true horseman at work on the range. His horse will work for him all day long without a bobble.

Above all, due to its sensitivity, the rider must take great care of his horse's mouth. Why is a horse with a decent mouth so seldom found? Because riders have not taken the time to develop the mouth and understand its connection with the horse's movements. Light hands of rider, light mouth of horse; good hands, good mouth; educated hands, beautiful mouth.

It takes months and years to develop educated hands. They are acquired only after a rider has learned to think when on a horse; to think, to consider, to understand what each action of his body, and above all his hands, asks or commands the horse to do.

Tell your students to look at their hands. What do they see? Hands that are thin and graceful; hands large and big-boned; nervous hands; quiet hand; old — young — brown — white hands. All different in appearance. But within those hands are the secret of horsemanship. Those hands touch the reins. (See Methods of Holding Reins.) (Illus. 10, 10a)

Hands are what make a rider great or mediocre. Every movement, almost every thought of a horse can be felt through educated hands.

Ill. 9

Asking for the back. The action here is resistance of the horse being met by equal resistance of the rider's hand. When the horse relaxes his mouth or poll, the hand will relax. The close-up shows how little movement is done by the rider's wrist and fingers to ask for the back. The original position of the hand was up about two inches, the thumb and forefinger in a straight line with the wrist and arm. In the close-up, notice the little finger position and the slight change of hand and fingers in 9 and 9a.

Ill. 9a

Schooling

Showing
(One Finger Between Reins)

Ill. 10

Combination

California

Showing
(No Finger Between Reins)
Ill. 10a

51

Chapter IV

MOVEMENTS

There are only eight basic movements for the Western horse, although there are variations of these movements. For instance, the serpentine is a variation of the half-circle.

The eight basic movements are:

1. Stop
2. Back
3. Leads
4. Circles
5. Flying Change
6. Rollback
7. Offset or Pivot
8. Spin

Encourage your pupils to bear in mind why the movements of the Western horse are what they are. All are for the purpose of getting a job done, whether cutting, roping, riding fence, or barrel racing. Ground lost, motion wasted, is time lost, money down the drain. The movements are not necessarily valued by the clock, as to how fast they are, but, rather, as to how handy they are. Did they avoid losing ground?

This chapter will discuss both the movements and proper methods of schooling for them.

However, the teacher should bear in mind that, while a proper understanding of schooling should be given to intermediates, generally the schooling of a horse is beyond any but advanced students. The present chapter, therefore, applies to both intermediate and advanced courses. How far intermediate students can go in schooling for execution of the movements is a matter of the individual classes and riders, and the teacher's decision.

The Stop (Ill. 11-15)

The first movement that a horse is taught and that a rider should learn is — to stop. This is one of the most exasperating, the most often required and frequently the most poorly executed of all the movements.

How should a horse stop?

He should stop in a balanced position, ready to move again, whether to jump forward, roll back, back, or even spin. Many times a horse, after a hard, fast stop, is about as ready for motion as a thousand pound log stuck in the mud.

No two horses stop the same way. One may run down and just cease motion. Another slides. Still another freezes in a squat.

Which is best?

To my mind, if a horse can travel at speed, stop in a given area and still be prepared to continue a movement, then, whether that stop is balanced or sliding, if it is "soft" to the rider and done correctly as far as the horse's head, neck and body are concerned, it is a good stop in the style of that individual horse.

Let the rider ask himself, "Can I immediately move my horse where I want him? Is he set, ready to go? Or is he just a stick, with his feet rooted in the ground?"

If he is not ready to go, the stop is no good, regardless of how fast or how showy it was.

Ill. 11

The Stop. This is the beginning of a nice, smooth, well balanced stop. The whole attitude of the horse is one of quietness, obedience. The horse's mouth is closed. The rider's right rein has a little more slack than the left. She is down in the saddle with her hips, leg position is good. The position of her upper body is with the stop.

The position of the horse's body in a stop may vary in individual horses. But essentially it is: mouth relaxed, head in vertical or near-vertical position, poll relaxed, neck perhaps 15° or more from withers (this last governed by natural neck-set on withers), the loins slightly convex and relaxed, the hindquarters well up under the

53

Ill. 12

The Stop. Because of the angle of this shot and the importance of the stop, two pictures are included. This one shows more action and was done at greater speed. The horse's hocks are low to the ground, the angle of the stifle has closed, as has the angle at the hock. The back of the horse's top line has acquired a convex profile; the face of the horse is vertical, his neck is arched, his mouth closed. There is a little too much contraction of the rider's leg.

horses's body. Some horses even carry their hind feet up under their cinches.

In intermediate teaching, show the class a good stop at speed. (Note: Be sure to use soft ground to stop in. The bounce is not always the rider's or horse's fault. It may be that the horse is merely trying to protect himself). Let the students see the demonstration several times, while you comment on good head set, effect of light hands, soft mouth, timing (right or wrong), and so no.

Then, not at speed, demonstrate how to obtain this stop. Walk and stop. Walk and stop.

Let a top student, or one from you radvanced class, give a class demonstration. Then call out an intermediate student to walk and stop, walk and stop, while you comment, until the horse stops light in the hand and does not poke his nose either out or toward the ground. If a horse does either of these things, he is resisting the bit and stopping on the front legs. A horse light in the hand does not stop on his forehand.

In all movements, it is necessary to remember that the hindquarters can handle weight, movement and speed, while the forehand is but the prop.

Ill. 13
The Stop. Here's what can happen through incorrect timing!

Ill. 14

(Three nationally known judges in A.H.S.A. and A.Q.H.A. made their critique of the movements on each horse and rider. The judges are A, B and C.)

STOP

HORSE. A: No flexion in horse's poll, otherwise very good stop.

B: Quarters and hocks well under horse taking weight off forehand, poll a little stiff. Nose should be down, neck arched. Position of head and neck prevents convexing of loins and relaxation.

C. Horse is resisting slightly. No flexing at the poll.

RIDER. A: Position good, (with the momentum of speed it would have been hard to be in the saddle at this particular instant).

B: Rider's seat should be in saddle. Lower leg in good position to engage hindquarters. Rein hand soft.

C: Rider is in very good position.

Ill. 15

STOP

A: Horse looks as though he stumbled, he was caught at the wrong time by the rider, he tried to obey the aids to stop at the moment she asked for the stop and only succeeded in almost falling completely down.

B: Looks like a lunge forward. All weight of the horse is forward on the forehand; no engagement of hindquarters. Looks as if he had tried to engage hindquarters and stop but can't in trying to catch himself from falling.

C: Appears that this horse when pictured stumbled and has just regained his feet when picture was snapped as this was supposed to be a stop. Not much of a stop here. A horse cannot stop with his head lower than his withers.

Rider A: Stiff. She did have enough sense to give her horse a little rein when he stumbled.

B: Position in saddle good. Lower leg too far away from horse, toe too far out. Rein hand and arm nicely relaxed.

C: I would not criticize the rider of this horse. Perhaps she prevented a bad fall by taking hold of her horse in the manner shown.

Back
Back (Ill. 16-21)

The back is the only movement to the rear. When the back is correctly executed, the horse's feet step backward on the same two-beat as in the trot forward, with just a split-second's difference in the diagonal placing making it almost a four-beat.

The correct aids for backing are to "give" and "take" with the hands, this in timing with the steps of the horse's front legs, the rider's hand closing as the horse's left foot hits the ground, relaxing immediately; and checking, or closing, again when each foot strikes the ground.

Ill. 16

Back: Though the position of the horse's hindquarters shows that he is relaxed and backing readily and quietly, there is a slight resistance in the poll area, the face could be a little more vertical and the area around the throat latch and poll more relaxed. The position of horse and rider good. Note the lowering of the croup area and that the croup is lower than the withers.

Speed backward develops from a mere step backward of the green horse to the speed of the finished horse. The position of the horse's head and neck depends greatly on the natural neck-set on the withers. Neck should be arched, with flexion at the poll, mouth and jaw. Only through relaxed jaw and poll can this movement be successfully executed. The face of the horse should not be past the vertical. In profile, it is seen that the horse's hindquarters have dropped under his body.

It is difficult for some horses to back quickly because they are inclined to drop their hind legs so far under them that they are stepping on their hind feet with their front feet.

When beginning to school a horse to back, the rider may use one of the following aids:

(1) A resisting hand, giving the same tension at which the horse is resisting at the mouth, lightening the fingers instantly when the horse relaxes his jaw or takes a step backward. One or two steps is sufficient at first.

Ill. 17

Back: The horse looks like it is ready for anything but the back! There is no relaxation about the horse anywhere, the mouth is forced open, the jaw, poll and neck are rigid and in turn the hindquarters are locked. The rider has pulled herself forward out of the saddle, bowed her back, is grabbing with her lower calf to keep from falling forward and has a rigid set hand with no sympathy. Note incorrect head and eye position of rider.

Ill. 18

BACK

Horse A: Beginning the back, right after a stop. This shows collection after a balanced stop; horse is ready to do anything.

B. Horse at attention. Looks as if he is settling after a quick stop, preparing himself to back. Horse in this position is often referred to as gathered. Ready to go in any direction or at any speed asked for by the rider. Horse and rider's center of gravity in natural position. Horse's attention on rider.

C. Horse is backing very well. Rider has fine position. Horse flexed at poll and has given to rider's desire.

Rider A: Seat, hand good. Relaxation of rider shows in little finger

B. Rider has horse under complete control. She has soft sensitive fingers, body in perfect balance. Rider and horse one physical and mental unity.

C. Rider has very good position hands feet and seat are right to get the most performance out of the horse.

60

Ill. 19

A: Frozen. Open mouth. No flexion, feet planted solid.

B: Horse appears as if he has never been taught to back, resists all efforts. Rigid from head to tail. Opens mouth only to relieve the pain from the pull on the reins. Five minutes on the ground would help loosen up his poll.

C: This picture shows a horse that is not going to do any thing very good. The horse has his mouth wide open and is apparently frozen to the ground, as far as a back is concerned.

A: Rider frozen also. If she cut her reins, she'd fall off; if she cut her stirrup straps, she'd fall fall off! All of her weight is on her reins and stirrups.

B: Tyro (beginner) rider. Has been asked to back the horse when she herself doesn't know the technique and aids. Weight in wrong direction. Pulling on reins instead of intermittent signals of fingers. Pulling shouldn't be in a horseman's vocabulary.

C: The rider has very poor position she is humped over forward and there is no rythm between horse and rider. There is no flexion between the horse's mouth and the rider.

Ill. 20

Back Ill. 20

A. Horse has no flexion in poll. If there were more flexion there could be more action of the legs. Quarters are well up under him.

B: Horse has not learned to fully trust rider, does not want to back, but rider's aids and insistance, softly and tactfully given, induces horse to go back readily but somewhat reluctantly as evidenced in raised neck, stif neck, poll and concave loins. Evidently a young or unschooled horse, but one that shows excellent promise in schooling with tact from rider.

C: The only thing that I see wrong with this back is flexion of the horse's poll to the pull of the rider.

A. Good .

B. Position of rider in complete harmony with balance of horse. Lower leg engaging horse's hindquarters. Soft, supple hands signaling horse with fingers, very slight traction on reins.

C: Rider position is very good.

Back Ill. 21

This mare is completely relaxed, look at her ears, head, neck position, — look at the rider's hands. All ready for a proper back.

(2) Lightly play with the left and right rein by closing the fingers. The light play relaxes the horse's mouth.

(3) A third method is to take a feel of the horse's mouth with a set hand, closing the legs and forcing the horse to go into the bit and relax his jaw.

In teaching a horse to back, various developments to be avoided include:

(1) The skip or hop backward
(2) Backing sideways
(3) Bending of the horse's body.

Causes of these undesirable developments are:

(1)   Skipping backwards results from too heavy a hand on the bit and from improper introduction of the horse to backing. Hopping and skipping backward indicate fear of the hands and lead to rigid neck muscles which in turn freeze the hindquarters. The horse tries to protect his mouth by freezing his jaw and poll. This freezes neck and hindquarters.

(2) and (3)   Backing crookedly, or with the horse's body bent, also comes from the rider's asking the horse to back faster than his training so far has qualified him to do. What is happening is that the hindquarters are not moving as fast as the hands are asking through the mouth. Something has to give. Result: Backing crookedly, or bending of the horse's body, generally at the base of the neck.

Too often a rider attempts to get a horse to back by jabs on the rein, which are as meaningless to the horse as are senseless jabs with the spur.

Some horses will respond to the use of a squeezing leg to accelerate the back, where another horse will either become confused or resist.

Know your horse.

Circle and Half-Circle

Circle and half-circle should be done with the horse's body curved to follow the arc of a circle, whether at walk, jog, lope or any speed. Hindquarters should not be outside nor the shoulder inside the arc of the circle. Impress on pupils: *"Horse's head and eye should always point in the direction in which he is going. Let him see where he is going. Your own neck is what you risk if you don't."*

Circle and half-circle are elementary movements and are generally among the first asked of a horse.

Some horses are so stiff on a longitudinal line that it is necessary to limber up their bodies by working simple circles and half circles. Such a horse probably travels with his hindquarters to the outside of the circle.

To correct, use outside leg in No. 2, "behind the cinch," position.

To correct a horse that drops his forehand or shoulder to the inside of the circle, use inside leg at cinch, and, if the horse is on snaffle or hackamore, use inside No. 2 rein.

The ability of a horse to bend properly to the circle is vital for changing leads and for the rollback, for barrel racing, and for cutting and roping in the arena and on the range.

The horse is an athlete and, as such, should be supple, well balanced and coordinated so that he can control any part of his body at any time. A horse that is flexible and coordinated is the rider's to command, anywhere, at work or at show.

Proper rider position for taking the circle: Rider shifts weight to his own inside hip, with the weight shift as much or as little as speed of horse and size of circle demand.

Leads (Ill. 22-28)

The movement called leads takes its name from the fact that at the lope a horse has a leading foot. Left forefront leading is "left lead;" right forefoot leading is "right lead."

Almost all horses running free in the pasture will take a correct lead through their own natural sense of balance. However, the weight of the rider disrupts this natural sense of balance, and, in general, a horse under the saddle must be re-taught the when and where of leads.

Correct leads: Turning to the left, a horse should take the left lead; to the right, the right lead.

For this reason, one of the main aids is the rider's outside leg in No. 2 position, which controls the horse's hindquarters, urging them to the inside.

The hand aids, to begin with, should be: Inside rein raised very slightly and approximately in No. 3 reining position. This brings the horse's shoulders upright, curving the neck and bringing the nose slightly to the inside. The upright shoulder frees the inside foreleg.

Correct aids for right lead: Use left leg at No. 2, inside leg at No. 1; rein slightly raised in approximately No. 3 position. The tilt of the horse's head inward should be no more than enables the rider to see the corner of the horse's eye.

Incorrect riding in this movement may result in a disunited horse or in putting the horse into a false, or outside, lead.

"Disunited" means left lead in front, right lead behind, or vice versa. This makes for very rough and uncoordinated action, loss of efficiency, time and ground.

To correct: Use outside leg with intermittent pressure to put the hindquarters to the inside; or check and bring horse to a trot and start over with aids for the left lead.

The outside, or false, lead can be dangerous. If a horse is on the outside lead, say, right lead, when turned left, he is apt to cross his feet and go down.

To correct: Check horse to a jog and give correct aids; or use outside leg to check the horse so he will not increase his pace, then ask for a flying change. A horse that has been given preliminary schooling on obedience to leg aids, to move the hindquarters left or right at pressures from the rider's leg at No. 2, or to the right if rider's left leg presses at No. 2, will understand readily what is being asked for.

Change of Leads Ill. 22

Horse A: Horse is maintaining a left lead in a right hand circle.

B: Horse is galloping false, not strain in position, maybe due to rider's failure to use left leg back and vigorously.

C: There was no change of leads here.

Rider A: Too far forward.

B: Rider's seat and attitude go

C: Rider's position is a little far forward.

Flying Change of Leads Ill. 22-28)

A perfect change of leads is executed as the horse is rolling ov his leading foot. Immediately after this, the horse goes into a su pension, where all four feet are off the ground. Only at this time it possible for him to change leads of all four feet *simultaneously*.

The change of leads for the Western horse should come wh the direction changes. Some horses are more adept at this change leads than others and need little schooling to perfect the moveme Other horses need it drilled into them.

There are several methods for schooling the flying change.

First of all, the horse must be able to take either lead from walk, from a halt, and even from a back. Only when he is through

Change of Leads Ill. 23

Horse A: Horse changed behind first and is just beginning to come into left lead in front. The horse has a right lead behind but in the next phase will make a change in back. The rider has obviously caught the horse off guard, for there is no lead in front. The action will be, hind leg change then front. (It should be simultaneous).

B: Appears leads are confused. In requesting a change of leads, the timing for aids is paramount for a smooth change. Timing here is off. Horse, in a stride or two, will apparently come into the proper lead. However, rider is depending primarily on rein aids to get change rather than dropping lower right leg back sooner till lead is accomplished.

C: This change of leads is going to be the natural front first then the hind. A very good looking change to me.

Rider A: Reining too high, a little hard. No use of legs.

B: Rider position excellent, rein aid too obvious, hand too wide. Rider well in balance with horse.

C: Rider position is good.

Change of Leads Ill. 24

Horse A: Relaxation, but alertness apparent in mare. The acquiesence of mare very appealing. Almost perfect coordination between horse and rider. Mare working as if she were free, no resentment whatsoever.

B: Picture caught with left hind leg on ground, a smooth balanced alert lope with right lead. Horse is alert and ready for any signal. Rider has approached camera on left lead had given aids for right; this appears to be first stride of a simultaneous change to the right lead.

C: Rider has asked for the change of lead from the left to the right and is getting it through leg and rein aid. This change will be both front and back at the same time. A very good change that takes a lot of schooling to get on a horse. I don't recommend this change for green horses and or riders.

Rider A: Bareback and with only a mane hold, the rider would still be in the same position. You can't help calling it quite a good position.

B: Position of lower left leg against horse and rider's weight slightly to right confirm these comments. Position good.

C: Rider positions the horse very well for this change.

Change of Leads Ill. 25

This mare has just made a simultaneous change of leads, this is the first stride of her change to the left lead. Note the position of head and neck, slightly to the left, and the completely relaxed attitude of the animal. The rider is erect and supple in her saddle, hand light — there is no exaggerated change in body position. Looks like harmony on horse back.

schooled to this point should the rider attempt schooling for lead change.

Change of leads can be asked for in reverse or half-turn in reverse. Always try to make the horse wait for you to make the change. (See Fig. 4, with the correct change being at X on the finished horse).

Wide and easy serpentines, or riding in wide open country with plenty of room to change, are helpful in this phase of training.

At any time of schooling, be sure the horse fully understands the aids.

Faults to watch for are:
(1) Anticipating
(2) Disuniting
(3) Outside lead
(4) No lead in back, particularly in circles, i.e., the horse is galloping with both hind feet moving as one.

Change of Leads Ill. 26

This horse has a right lead in back, left lead in front, is almost grabbing the right fore with the right hind. His mouth is open, too much rein action, reins too high on neck. The rider has slumped in the saddle is carrying the reins and reining shoulder too far forward, the whole upper body is twisted. She is giving no help to the horse or indication of what she wants except from the reins and rein hand. Almost everything is obviously wrong here. Neither horse or rider seem to understand what is required. Open mouth on horse. Disunited, the horse will probably have to break to a trot to get a correct lead. Riders reins too tight and high left shoulder, and upper body are trying to tell the horse to go right and change leads, but their is no help from the legs, or weight. Should be sitting straight up from hip to shoulder instead of slumped and twisted.

First teach the horse his leads at a given point, working toward habit. Then, if necessary, bring him into several strides at a jog, then at a hesitation, and ask for the other lead.

Correction of the outside, or false, lead and of disuniting have already been discussed.

No lead in back is an incorrect action which few people are able to detect. As a rule, the horse is moving at speed on a circle or figure 8 when the fault occurs. Its possible causes are slippery ground, anticipation of lead change, and attempt of the horse to maintain his balance. To correct, particularly in the case of a green horse, slow up. Give the horse better footing — plow up your ground, if you have to. The horse is afraid of slipping.

Change of Leads Ill. 27

The camera has caught this horse at a good time for illustrating. Both hind feet are off the ground and one can see that the right hind is beginning to drop further under the horse's body as it should do for the right lead; at the next half stride the right fore should shift and take the right lead. This is called a hind leg change first. Horse should have made a simultaneous change; rear, them front, is second best. Generally results from rein aid before leg aid. Ears of horse not good. Rider with knee slightly too high, otherwise position and attitude good. Left rein too much tighter than right, by the change, rider used reins before leg for change of leads.

On your lead changes, do not punish the horse so severely th‥ he anticipates because of fear of punishment. A horse cannot wo﹖ with confidence if he fears either slippery footing or a punishi﹖ rider. His uncertainty will show in his work.

In giving the aids, unless you are an experienced and high﹖ skilled trainer with a keen sense of timing, do not expect a horse﹖ change leads as soon as you give the aids. Allow time for the hor﹖ to understand what you want. Give the aid. Let the horse set hi﹖ self, then make the change.

A well schooled horse can make a change of leads in the bridl﹖ on a contact rein, a loose rein, or from weight.

Change of Leads Ill. 28

This picture was included to show a horse making the change of leads i﹖ front before taking it behind. The mare has a right lead in front and a le﹖ lead behind, at the next period when the hind feet are off the ground sh﹖ completed the change. It should be remembered that in the change o﹖ leads there is always a period when the rider can do nothing but upse﹖ the horse if he asks a horse to change i.e., here, there is nothing the ride﹖ can do now to make the horse take the change of leads simultaneousl﹖ with the front feet, short of tying onto a helicopter and elevating th﹖ hindquarters. Don't abuse the animal with whip or spur if your timin﹖ has been incorrect. If you have asked for the change of leads. Now wa﹖ for the horse to complete it. (The rider's left leg is positioned for righ﹖ lead.)

72

Figure 8's

A figure 8 is a tricky movement. It is a combination of the circle and the leads. It is used in the reining pattern to show a horse's ability to change his leads at the proper point. In a horsemanship pattern, it is used to show the rider's ability to get the change of leads at the proper time.

Although figure 8's are simple, it is not often that a correct execution of this movement is seen.

Figure 8's may be worked slow or fast, small or large. The faster the speed, the more inclination (due to gravity) will the horse have to lean toward the inside of the circle.

If a rider knows his circle and leads, he will find that the figure 8 is nothing more than putting two circles together, with a change of leads at the intersection of the circles.

Aids: The inside stirrup is almost invariably weighted. Depending on the degree of schooling of the horse, the change will be

(1) From habit

(2) From weight

(3) From leg and rein aids.

Very often in (1) we run into anticipation, with the horse ducking his circle.

In (2), the horse will often give a front lead change before hind leg. At best, he is half a stride off.

Except on a well-schooled horse, it is usually better to ask for the lead change with your leg aid, either simultaneously with weight and rein or before, since the leads originate from the hindquarters.

In the case of some few horses which are extremely well balanced, you will see a change in back half a stride before a change in the fore legs, even when these horses are at liberty.

In order to avoid anticipation, the trainer should continue to work circles, not only to give the horse a feel of the circle and balance, but to let the horse know that all circles are not the beginning of a figure 8.

As a schooling measure, often the best way, assuming you are working in the arena, is to make your horse change in the middle and go all the way out to the fence before changing direction.

73

Rollback

Rollback (Ill. 29-34)

The rollback is a 180° pivot *on the hindquarters*, the horse r◖ turning in the tracks on which he came up. The rollbacks, of a◖ the movements can save the most ground, gain the most time.

A horse going up on a left lead should check and rollback to th◖ right, coming out on a right lead. The check and turn on the finishe◖ horse are one movement.

The reason the horse comes out on the inside lead is that he ha◖ dropped his inside foot under him to catch his weight, and, in thi◖ position, the hind legs, as a pivot, have already set the forelegs fo◖ the lead. The horse will hold that lead if his hindquarters do n◖ move or flip. The line of the horse's body from ear to tail is more c◖

Roll Back Ill. 29

There are essentially three phases to the roll back; a. the decrease in speed◖ or check; b. the roll back over the hocks; c. the break, or break-away◖ Picture above, the mare is starting the check, though on the whole giving a◖ very relaxed appearance for this very strenuous movement. Notice th◖ dust the left hind foot is stirring up, the mare's head, neck, attitude al◖ are correct and very good. She has a deceptive way of making everything◖ appear as if it were simple and easy.

less a curve, with the nose and head leading the body. Some horses work in a straight line, with the forehand coming up and around. The hindquarters are the hinge of the gate, the forehand is the opening side.

Though some authorities feel that a horse should come up in a right lead to turn left, there are some horses that, regardless of which lead they come up in, in their checking or slowing down movement, are in no lead. They will then take the lead in whichever direction the rider asks.

Roll Back Ill. 30

Here is the beginning of the roll back, this horse has come in with a good check, from the rider's weight shift and aids, the horse has dropped the left hind foot slightly deeper under his body, the roll back is to the left. Here the left fore foot is beginning to slightly lead the right fore. Horse will also have the left lead in front. Except for the little twist in the horse's head, which is due to too much rein, the position of the horse is good and correct. It would have been better if the horse had led slightly with his head to the left. Except for too much rein, a little too far over and across the neck, rider position is correct.

In the schooling procedure for the rollback, it is best to start at the walk. Check your horse to get him on his hindquarters. Tap him with your outside leg at No. 1. Use your rein lightly at No. 3 to the inside, mostly to keep the horse from going forward.

In the beginning, ask your horse only to take one or two steps around the hindquarters, which is about a 45° angle. Then let him walk off, which is your way of saying "thank you" to him.

Not until a horse can do a 180°, or even a 360° pivot, quietly and smoothly at the walk, do you take him to the jog.

At the jog, the horse has to halt before he makes his pivot, since he cannot trot around at the rollback. Only when the horse can do it well at jog do you ask for the lope.

At all gaits, if a horse can maintain his tranquillity, we leave the rollback at the gait he came into it — in other words, walk up, walk away; jog up, jog away; lope up, lope away. But — repeat — do this only if he is quiet.

Roll Back Ill. 31

Notice the action in this phase. The horse is breaking off at speed, turning to the left, she has already the left lead behind and by the time the forehand has hit the ground she will have it in front. The mare has her head and neck toward the direction she is going. The rider's upper body is with the thrust of the hind leg — there is a straight line from the right hock of the mare through the rider's seat, trunk and shoulders. From the angle of the shot, it appears as if the right hand were covering the horn, but it is not. The rider's right leg is back asking for the left lead.

There are several other ways to school for the rollback, assuming that horse has had sufficient basic schooling. One is to make a circle tangent to the arena fence. Where the circle to the right meets the fence, ask the horse to turn back left. Thus you are using the fence as an aid. Horse should go out on a left lead.

Vice versa on this procedure for the left.

Another way is to check on the fence, turning or rolling the horse to the fence. But, after you feel the horse is working this way to your satisfaction, be sure to start working him away from the fence.

One reason for working on the fence is to give the horse a feel of the movement without the rider having to over-use the aids, for which the fence is a substitute.

Possible faults in the rollback:

    (1)   Slipping of the hindquarters
    (2)   Turning on the forehand
    (3)   Turning on the middle
    (4)   Circling
    (5)   Coming out on the wrong lead.

To correct:

    (1)   Use your outside leg at No. 2 to hold the hindquarters so they will not move out of their pivot point.

    (2)   Not only is turning on the forehand incorrect, it is dangerous. The horse's hindquarters are so constructed that they can handle weight and pivot with weight. If the turn is made on the forehand, then we have one front leg as pivot point and stand the risk of a snapped pastern. Besides this danger, there is also a full length of distance lost, if time is a factor.

Correction: Teach the rider exactly what the rollback is. If the fault under discussion has occurred, the rider has asked the horse to change direction without checking to bring him on his hindquarters and probably has used only the rein aid up high on the neck. The correction is to check the horse, use the No. 3 rein aid and No. 1 leg aid.

    (3)   Here the horse has used his middle as pivot point instead of his hindquarters. Again this almost always is caused by the rider's using neck rein too high and no leg aid; or it may be that thehorse is over-tired.

Use same correction as for (2).

    (4)   Circling, too, is generally a rider fault. If this occurs, the rider has no understanding of what a rollback is and has merely tried to change directions without allowing the horse to come back to his hindquarters.

Correction: Know what a rollback is. And how to use correct aids.

Roll Back Ill. 32

Horse A: Too high and too much neck rein, hindquarters are under him as good as you would want any horse to have them.

B: Appears as if horse is coming in with an excellent stop and start for the roll back. Stiff in the poll, neck too high; however there is good evidenc of convex loins Practically all of weight on hocks, which are almost touching the ground. The horse coming out of roll back on the proper lead. Horse appears sensitive to aids, as evidenced by flexed rein and wrist of rider.

C: Horse's feet are in good position. Horse's head is too high and is resisting the rider. Nose should be to the inside of the turn.

Rider A: Legs good, seat correct, I think the horse had not been working and the rider really set him down this trip.

B: Seat and legs in good position, rider's weight on inside bone of seat in direction of turn, upper body in unity with hore's body.

C: Rider position is good.

Roll Back Ill. 33

A: Too much neck rein. Hind-quarters are under him and ready.

B: Check is good on the left lead, rider has started aids for roll back, although riders hands are soft and aid given is good the horse is turning nose outwards and mouth is partly opened. There is undue stress shown in shoulder, neck area.

C: The roll back is started good. The horse is resisting the rider and his nose is turned to the right instead of the left.

A: She is a little too far forward and ahead of her horse. Hand position down low is nice.

B: Riders lower leg good, position at this point should be seated to saddle in order to pin down with the weight the left hind leg.

C: Rider has let her seat bounce up out of the saddle if the horse really rolls back the rider will not be with the horse when he comes out of the roll back.

Roll Back Ill. 34

A: Poor picture, timing just a fraction off, caught him spraddle legged behind. The horse's attitude shows he is not incorrect. Possible first check, and next instant would have been right to come around.

B: The horse has resisted aids in this check as evidenced by spraddled hind legs, concavity of loins. He is tight, although rider has not exerted strong rein aids. A green horse not yet sure what is wanted.

C: Roll back at this intsant it is very awkward for him to maneuver his legs into position to roll back. You have to roll to the opposite of the lead to get a good roll back. When a horse rolls to the left he comes out in a left lead and when to the right he comes out of the roll in the right lead.

A: Position good, maybe a little stiff possibly from the stop movement.

B: Seat and leg firm. Good, excellent position weight correctly distributed to seat, calves and legs to heels.

C: Rider has too much pressure on the reins and the horse is resisting.

If a horse circles and it not a rider fault, bring the horse back to basic work, which will begin at teaching the rollback at a walk. Be sure the horse has the feel of the movement before proceeding further.

(5) This may be either a horse or a rider fault. It could be the rider's fault in that he has not held the hindquarters, if it is necessary, with the outside leg at No. 2. Some horses are so sensitive to a rider's weight shift that they may start on the correct lead, but, due to a slight weight shift by the rider, they may go back to the outside lead to stay under the rider's weight.

Correction: The rider should try to maintain correct weight placement and use outside (No. 2) leg aid.

In all movements, practice makes perfect. Remember, a tired horse easily becomes a rebellious horse.

Besides the rollback described here, there is the California rollback (if over 180°, the spin), the difference being that in the California "rollback" the horse, instead of checking after a straight rundown, comes to a halt, settles for several seconds, and then executes a 180° or more pivot and moves off in his original tracks.

Offset and Pivot (Ill. 35-37)

The offset or pivot is a 180° or 90° ($\frac{1}{2}$ or $\frac{1}{4}$) pivot or turn on the hindquarters, done from the halt, with the forehand coming up and around, as in the rollback. It is used to show the horse's handiness, lightness, and readiness to obey the aids.

Correct aids: Offset to the right calls for left rein in No. 3 position, bearing across the horse's neck, immobilizing the hindquarters and giving direction, and left leg at No. 1 moving the forehand. There is a slight weight shift to the horse's inside hip. The upper body of the rider should remain forward, in balance with the horse's movements.

It is interesting to note that some horses will position their hind legs together and are thus able to pivot right or left, with no lead in back.

Offset to the right should have a right lead. Offset to the left, left lead.

Look out for:
  (1) Turn on forehand
  (2) Turn on middle.

Corrections: Same as for these faults in the rollback.

Offset or Pivot Ill. 35

There is little or no difference between the spin and offset except the degree of the turn. The spin is 360° or more, the offset or pivot is 90° to 180°. Here we have pictures of the mare turning both left and right. in the first picture to the left notice how the left hind foot is dropped further under the body and that there is more weight on the left hind. She has dropped her croup, the hind legs are taking the preponderance of the weight and the forehand is being raised. She is leading with her head. A fraction of a second later the left fore will be ahead of the right fore. She has just touched the ground going to the right which meant a right lead; now offsetting to the left she will raise her forehand and the left fore will become the leading foot. Everything good — attitude, position of horse, rider. The right rein could be slightly lower.

Offset or Pivot Ill. 36

Here the mare is offsetting to the right, notice the change of position of the hind feet and how the right fore is deep under her body. The position is not quite as good as the preceding picture. She is coming from an offset to the left and still has the left fore as leading foot, at the next period of movement the right fore will become he leading foot. Head, neck position of mare good. Right rein could be a little lower. Position of rider good, is forward with movement of offset. Notice the light, relaxed hand and wrist in both pictures.

Offset or Pivot Ill. 37

Since there is great similarity between the spin and offset we are only using one picture here for critique.

A: I like this. Left leg stuck up under him where it is supposed to be shows a lot of action and suppleness not resisting one iota. Working off leg aids, rein is very light. Sum picture up by saying: shows action, balance, obedience, unity.

B: Horse offsetting to left, hocks well under him, pivoting on left hind, with left fore leg in lead. Horse relaxed, signals from rider soft light, horse fairly well relaxed in poll, this movement requires shortening of neck relaxing of poll to put weight back on hocks.

C: Horse is in a more nearly perfect position to do a really good spin or offset depending on whether you want to stop at the quarter turn or half or go clean on around.

Spin (Ill. 38-42)

The spin is a 360°, or more, pivot on the hindquarters, with the horse maintaining his pivot point and, in spinning to the right, maintaining the right lead; to the left, the left lead.

It should be possible to bring him out of the spin at any point on the same lead on which he came in.

This is one of the most difficult and complex movements in Western riding because the horse is required to move his bulk without the use of momentum. It is a movement very tiring for the horse. In schooling, the rider must use utmost discretion in asking the horse to make this movement. A horse over-tired learns many defenses in this particular movement.

Spin Ill. 38

This is a very good looking spin This horse has his hind feet set well under his body with good weight distribution. Notice that there is more weight on the left hind (the left fetlock is closer to the ground), the croup is low, most of the horse's weight is on the hindquarters. The horse is beginning to raise the forehand, and it will be to the left lead. Horse is looking towards the direction it is going, body slightly bent in the withers-ars area. The rein could be a little lower. Notice the hand is not more than three inches from the horn . . . Rider position good for this period of the spin; in other words just getting started yet, an instant later the rider should be a little bit more forward.

Correct aids are the same as those for the pivot, except that the rider does not bring the horse out of the spin until he has gone a minimum of 360° around.

Possible faults:

  (1) Turn on the middle
  (2) Turn on the forehand
  (3) Sluggishness.

For (1) and (2), make the same correction as in rollback and in offset or pivot.

(3) Try to keep horse in front of the leg. Be sure he is in good enough condition to take this work.

Schooling in this movement begins with the horse doing pivots of progressively 90°, 180°, and finally 360° or more on the hindquarters, from a walk, jog and lope. Note that horse must cease the jog before pivoting.

Spin Ill. 39

The horse is not quite set to give a good spin, too much weight is on the left hind, too heavy a rein too high on the neck has caused the horse to tilt his nose to the outside and resist at he mouth and poll which affects the work ability of the rest of the body. The rider is out of position, leaning slightly right, although asking the horse to go left.

Circle left at lope. Pivot left, 360° at one point on the curve to inside of circle, keeping horse's hindquarters on the arc of the circle. Left lead must be maintained throughout movement. In circling right, horse must maintain right lead.

An alternate procedure is to begin a large circle at lope. Gradually bring circle down in size.

When near the middle, check horse slight at x to bring weight to hindquarters. At first, see if he can do even 45° of a 360° spin and maintain his lope. When he begins to lose momentum, let him ease back out of spin at lope and come out of the circle still on the left lead.

Spin Ill. 40

Horse A: Hindquarters correct, reins are slack, mare not resisting at all, the mare is working primarily off of leg aid.

B: Most of weight on left hind foot left fore leg is coming into position to lead right fore, head and neck are slightly bent in direction of movement, riders weight on left seat bone, right leg signals to keep up movement.

C: Horse has just started the spin to the left and his left front has not yet taken up the lead.

Rider A: Position good, weight is off of hindquarters.

B: Weight of rider from top of her head direct to point of hocks is in harmony with the mass of the horse.

C: Rider is using the leg aside to induce the horse to spin. Leg is too far to the rear, could be up a couple inches.

Very helpful in teaching the spin are 360° pivoting turns to the inside on a circle to the left, the horse maintaining left lead all the way around, with hindquarters in place and forehand loping around. In going around, the hindquarters spin and pivot. The horse's hindquarters are like the hinges of a gate.

Spin Ill. 41

Horse A: Hindquarters correct for next spin to right, but spraddle legged in front. Horse's attitude not resisting her, but he is going to get into a storm, can't help himself.

B: Horse starting spin to right, completely relaxed but timing and rhythm has forced him to start the spin on outside hind leg instead of right hind leg, technical fault.

C: Horse's feet are in a bad position to be well balanced.

Rider A: Rider reining too high.

B: Rider's weight even in saddle should be more on right seat bone. Position of rider good.

C: Riders reins are too long. The pull is too high on the horse's neck, and too far out to the right.

Spin Ill. 42

Horse A: Hindquarters are sure tucked under him. First impression is rider is fighting horse, but the more you study it the more nearly perfect it is, very light rein aid, resisting bit a little.

B: Horse is in fast spin, weight and pivot is right hind leg, and leading with right foreleg. Horse well balanced with weight on hocks.

C: Horse's front feet are too high off of the ground for a good spin. The spin is executed more on the flat plane rather than on too much of a set down and roll. A horse can not continue to spin when he is so high up in the front.

Rider A: Rider appears to be picking him up rather than reining him to the right. He'll get the best job done, though other two horses are quieter.

B: In excellent position with weight inside seat bone and distributed where her horse can use it best. Rein aid is a signal and not a pull across the horse's neck. Other side of picture would evidently show outside leg back and active.

C: Rider position is very good here.

Conclusion

All these eight movements are set down here in cold, hard words, but the instructor who teaches them to other riders must never forget to instill into his pupils' minds that a horse is not a machine; that each horse is different; and that the utmost tact should be used on every individual horse. Some animals will show natural talent for one movement or another.

There is no perfect horse, there can be no perfect rider. The goal is to reach as near perfection as the limitations of horse and rider will allow.

Chapter V

SUPPLING EXERCISES

Exercise in the saddle, to promote suppleness and confidence, are important, not only to beginning riders but to intermediate and advanced classes as well.

Slow, easy gymnastics, to warm up horse and rider, correspond to do-re-mi of the singer, or the warm-up of the pitcher before a ball game.

What is the specific function of these exercises? To ride at his best, a horseman must have control of any part of his body, both in conjuction with or independent of the rest of his body. No physical activity requires more complete coordination than horsemanship, for not only must a rider coordinate his own body and reactions but he must transmit his wishes to his partner, the horse. If a rider does not transmit his wishes intelligibly to the horse, through the aids — legs, weight, voice and hands — the result is confusion. And confusion can become chaos.

What rider would "ask" his horse to rear, jig, bolt?

The contradictory "asking" is not conscious on the rider's part, of course. But a well-trained horse has been taught all his life to obey man. Let us say this horse is trying to receive signals. "Run!" says the too-tight leg. "Stop!" say the reins.

The horse knows nothing but to obey — and the commands are in opposition! He becomes confused. Confusion leads to irritation and fright. Who was at fault?

Suppling exercises, developing smooth coordination and control on the part of the rider, help prevent such deplorable and dangerous situations.

Of course, a sensitive control does not come to a rider without practice. And few riders now-days can devote the endless hours to riding that, under ideal conditions, should be given.

The following suppling exericses are a substitute for all the time that a rider should, but cannot, spend in the saddle.

The parts of the rider's body most important in riding are ankles, knees, hip joints, loins, shoulders, neck, elbow and fingers. These exercises help each of these parts to perform its proper function and allow the horseman to ride without giving conscious thought to their coordination.

1. Exercise for Ankles

    Most common fault to be corrected: stiffness, which in turn affects the heel position and the rider's ability to retain the stirrup. (The ability to lower the heel, of course, answers the problem of standing on the toe or ball of the foot).

Rotate the ankle, up, down and around, in a circular movement, clockwise with the right foot, counterclockwise with the left foot.

Flex the ankle up and down, up and down.

Both movements should be done slowly, regularly, with conscious endeavor to keep the rest of the body quiet and the general position and seat undisturbed.

2. Exercise for Knees.

Common fault: lack of suppleness and strength.

Move the leg below the knee back toward the horse's hips until the foot is horizontal with the knee. Then return the foot smoothly to normal position.

3. Exercise for Thighs.

Common fault: heavy muscles of the thigh bone rest on the saddle, contributing to a poor seat.

Move the thigh out and away from the horse until the leg is about one foot behind the stirrup. Allow the leg to return to the side of the horse.

Draw the thigh forward until it is in normal position. From this movement, which is only done at a halt, the teacher may take his riders into the faster gaits. If they lose seat or leg, return to the halt and repeat the thigh movement.

4. Exercise for Loins.

Common fault: stiffness.

To combat this rigidity, there are several excises for rotation:

a) With right (or left) arm shoulder high, pretend a glass of water is in the upturned palm. Carry the arm from front to rear, slowly, rotating the body from the waist or loin.

b) Repeat, with both arms up at the same time, opposite each other, i.e., one over horse's neck while the other is over the croup.

c) With reins in one hand, touch horse on left shoulder, then on right hip, reaching over the rein hand. Note that the body from waist down should be as motionless as possible. (Illus. 44)

d) Raise the thighs, right, then left, then both, upon command. (Illus. 44a)

It is interesting to take a good group of riders into the lope, having them still maintain their position, except for a slight backward shift of the body. Thus, they are in almost the exact position of a bareback bronc rider, balanced on the seat, with a flexed loin.

The instructor should not require any of these movement for too long a time.

5. Exercise for Shoulders.
   Common fault: contraction of the shoulder muscles.
   Raise the right arm straight upward.
   Carry the arm down to the side, up and around, making a verticle circle.
   Be sure the movements are steady and smooth.

6. Exercise for Neck.
   Common fault: rigid unyielding neck.
   Look up slowly; then down slowly.
   Or, look as far to the left as possible, then to the right.

Note that all six exercises are not only for the coordination of muscles but for the separate control of each part, making it independent of voluntary or involuntary movements of other parts of the body.

Suppling Exercises Ill. 43, 43a

Another exercise, which does not entirely belong in the suppling category, is riding in the standing position.

Upon command, riders stand in their stirrups.

Depending on their skill or advancement, they will either hold on to mane or saddle horn; barely touch one of these; or assume the position without use of such exterior help.

Riders first take this position at a halt. Then, according to their ability, walk, jog or lope.

The position sought for is a relaxed ankle, the heel down with weight on the stirrup, either slightly to the inside or straight across the ball of the foot. The leg should cling all the way down the saddle or horse's sides. The rider's buttocks are raised out of the saddle and he has a slight crouch in the knee and hip joints. His trunk is straight from hip to shoulder, with about a 10° incline from the vertical. The rein hand is free of the horse and saddle, although the free hand may be on the horse's mane or on the saddle horn, if this is needed to maintain balance. Head and eyes are up.

Rider will take this position on command of the teacher Commands are "Sit!" "Standing position!" or "In your stirrups!"

The purpose of this movement is manifold. First, due to his weight coming out of the saddle, the rider must take that weight through the leg, ankle and heel. This redistribution of weight causes the rider to assume the correct position without forcing, particularly if he can and does relax his ankle.

Key to this position is the ankle. Relaxed and flexible, it not only allows the heel to come down but acts as a shock absorber and keeps the rider's weight off the toe.

Note that it is not possible to have a relaxed ankle unless the rest of the body is also relaxed. With the ankle, heel and foot in good position, the leg almost automatically falls into correct position.

The use of this position also leads to use of the back and loin muscles, and to the ability of the rider to get up with his horse when the latter breaks forward for a fast movement.

With a good group of riders, the teacher can call "In your stirrups!" "Sit!" "In your stirrups!" and have the commands executed smoothly for as long as he wishes. Such a group of riders can also take the standing position and hold it in all gaits, at all speeds or decrease of speeds, and in simple movements like circle, reverse, halt, and back.

This exercise is good to correct any position peculiarities from the seat down. Invariably, the teacher will find that when he takes a student back to sitting position after standing in the stirrups, the student's seat at least for a few minutes, is in correct position and balance.

It is surprising how many supposedly advanced riders cannot do the simplest of the foregoing exercises without grabbing the saddle horn or losing leg or hand position.

Some riders, of course, can do them more satisfactorily. If these consider themselves beyond the exercises, make a game out of an exercise session. Actually put a glass of water in the palm of these confident riders and work them all the way up to a gallop. Also test them in the standing position exercise, making it a rule that when the rider has to grab mane or sit down, he comes into the middle of the ring.

A few such tests, along with a logical explanation of the need of the exercises, will convince the class of their usefulness.

Emphasize that a rider may be in the advanced stage and still need suppling exercises, if for no other reason than that his ankle is still too stiff or his shoulders too tight.

Suppling exercises also increase a rider's confidence. Constriction of muscles is caused by a revolt of the nervous system stemming from fear. Fear cannot be overcome until the rider is at home on the horse.

Each exercise should be demonstrated and the teacher should give the reason for taking it. Comments should be short, and in terms easily understood.

After the demonstration, have each rider do the exercise individually. Then send the class to the rail to do it collectively, calling in any riders who need correction. If necessary, stop the whole class and ask one of them to demonstrate the exercise again. Ask for questions, if further explanation is needed.

Once convinced of the necessity for and importance of the exercises, a class will usually accept them wholeheartedly, derive much benefit from them, and enjoy their competitive and challenging elements.

Chapter VI

CLASS PROCEDURE

Class procedure, following the pattern of *demonstration, execution by students, evaluation, repetition*, should cover each movement until the teacher feels that the class is working to his satisfaction.

After the class can work the walk, jog, lope, reverse, circle, half-turn in reverse, halt and back, and can give a creditable pleasure-type or horsemanship-on-the-rail class performance, then introduce the eight movements progressively, repeating and going over them as extensively as the class requires. A new movement should not enter the picture other than very briefly until the prior movements are mastered.

Demonstrate (Ill. 45. a, b) and explain what you are after. Show the steps to obtain the desired results. Have each rider work with you individually for a few minutes until you feel he understands the movement and application of aids. If the class is large, work special students with the others as observers, then send the class to the rail and work them collectively.

The Check Ill. 45

Start the class working on each movement at a walk. Ask for halt, cautioning them to use the fingers to "give" and "take" and not to allow their horses to walk on after they have asked for the halt. Comment to individuals, if necessary. If the class as a whole is not working correctly on the movement, bring an individual into the middle and demonstrate again.

When you are satisfied with the majority of the work, advance the class to executing the movement at a jog, and on to the lope as they are ready. "Until they are ready" may mean one lesson; it may mean twenty lessons.

Class routine should not cover this or that movement only. Keep going back to the beginning, to give performance on the rail; to work on improving position; to apply the aids correctly; to take suppling exercises; and even to have the students take arena tests and use their skills in games.

Keep the class working, keep them interested, give them goals.

These goals might be set up by bringing in an expert rider to demonstrate barrel racing, cutting or reining.

The Rollback III. 45a

Breakaway   Ill. 45b

Another way to add variety and interest is to give the students a gymkahana, with the events set up with regard to their degree of skill.

Repeatedly during a lesson, ask the students to tell you the correct application of aids, what the correct position is for a movement, and why. Make them think.

A class, about mid-course, might go something like this:

(Scene: Your class ring. You are working your class in an enclosed area. Note: Only when you are sure of rider control will you allow them to work in an area that is not completely fenced or railed. The present class is one of twelve riders. They are all mounted and ready to begin.)

Teacher: Line up please. Before we start, we are going to go over a few basics. Let's begin with Pamela. Pam, tell me the correct position in the saddle.

Pam: (Any student should be very glib in this answer by now). Toes in; contact saddle with upper calf, knee and thigh; shoulders straight; uh — oh, I know — arms at

	side, with slight bend in elbow, hand relaxed; finger light and relaxed.
Teacher:	Is that all? Any one anything to add?
John:	Heels down
Teacher:	Where are you going to put your seat?
Anne:	(Raises her hand) In the middle of the saddle with a three point contact.
Teacher:	How about your head and eyes?
Class:	(In unison) Up!
Teacher:	Anything else? No? Well, I guess that's it . . . now, Bill give me the four aids.
Bill:	Leg, weight, voice, hands.
Teacher:	Very well . . . now, in this course we have covered the halt and the back. Today we will start on leads. Can anyone give the correct aids for the lead to the left?
Molly:	Outside leg.
Teacher:	Outside leg where?
Molly:	In No. 2 position.
Teacher:	Why?
Class:	(In unison) To move the horse's hindquarters to the inside.
	(Note: A class might, in fact *should*, answer this question in unison if the teacher has drilled this important point sufficiently into their minds.)
Teacher:	Are there any other aids?
Pam.	Use inside rein to turn horse's nose slightly to the inside Left leg at the cinch to tell the horse to take the lope and hold the shoulder from leaning in.
Teachers:	Is there a weight shift?
	(This question may cause a controversy. Teacher might explain as follows:)
	On a green, unschooled horse, it is necessary to use weight vigorously. On a schooled horse, the weight shift is only incidental to the whole movement. Do all of you understand the use of your aids? Now, while you stand in line, let me see you apply them.
	(Teacher quickly observes and corrects.)
Teacher:	John, please take the track to the right and demonstrate. I want you to demonstrate position and aids, giving the aids smoothly and tactfully. Ask your horse to jog. From the jog, take a lope.
	(Note: The value of sending one student to the rail is that the teacher can talk to the rest of the students during the demonstration. In other words, the eyes and ears of the students are both working.)

Teacher: (While John demonstrates) Did any of you observe his aids when he went from jog to lope?

(Various students try to answer. No real answers. Finally, agree on "No".)

Teacher: Notice his hand position, body position and leg and the quiet response of his horse . . . Ask him to walk, please, John . . . Now lope . . . (To class) You will notice that I am bringing him progressively down from the trot to the slower and more difficult gait. It is easier to go from a jog to a lope than it is to go from a walk to a lope . . . Halt, John . . . Lope . . . Again, you will notice the smoothness and immediate, smooth response of the horse . . . Walk, John, and halt your horse . . . Now back, and from the back take him into the lope . . . Ah! you notice here that the horse was unsure and had to go into forward motion before taking his lead . . . Too bad. Halt, please, John . . . (To class) John's demonstration as a whole was a logical sequence. In schooling your leads, do not ask your horse for a lead at the walk until he can do it readily at the jog, as John's horse did. If your horse falters at the walk, do more work on the leads from the jog. And be sure to work *both* ways of the ring . . . All right, John, ride in . . . You had a little trouble with your leads from the back into the lope. Do you know why?

John: Yes. I used my leg aids too fast and forgot which lead I was asking for.

Teacher: All right, then . . . Let's go to work. Class take the track to the left at a walk . . . Check your distance . . . All right . . . Jog . . . And lope . . . Before you ask the horse to take his lope, be sure he obeys your outside leg aid, thus showing that he understands which lead you are asking for. Then give the other aid, or aids, asking him to take the lope . . . Anne, wrong lead. Bring your horse back to a jog and give the correct aids, outside leg at No. 2 . . . Wait for him to obey that leg aid before you ask him to lope. Be sure he is set for the lope . . .

(Teacher observes if class procedure is good. If not, brings the whole class to a halt. Goes over aids again. And then asks class to jog. Calls each student in turn and asks him to take the leads. Continues to work any student who does his aids incorrectly before calling the next name. If one rider does not comprehend and is holding up the class, the teacher calls him into the center of the ring so he can watch while the teachers talks. This allows him

to observe while the teacher clarifies. When he thinks he
is ready, teacher sends him back to the ring.

If the class works well, the teacher asks them to take the
walk.)

When they come in, the teacher might stress a point he has
been making all through the course — that in executing all verbal
commands of the teacher, the student should take his time; the
teacher's command does not mean they are to obey *immediately*.
The transition from one gait to another should be smooth and very
quietly and tactfully done. If the horse is not ready, the rider must
wait.

During ring procedure, the teacher commends different students
frequently — "Fine, Barbara." "You are doing much better, Joe, your
position is good now." — and so on, taking care to spread the praise
as equally as possible over the whole class.

Toward the end of the lesson, the teacher, to add variety but
continue to impress the subject on the students, proposes a competition.

The whole class goes to the track. Teacher explains that anyone
who makes an incorrect lead is to come into the center of the ring
and help catch the others when they are at fault.

The class is worked progressively, starting from jog to lope, and
when a rider makes an error, he is called in. Teacher is commenting
to those called in while the ones on the rail still work.

The survivors go down the scale to the walk, halt, back, change
of direction; go up and down the gaits to the lope until all but one
student is eliminated.

He wins a coke!

Teacher dismisses them with: "That's all today. Any questions
on any of the work we have just done?"

If the class is alert, some riders certainly should pause to ask
questions as they ride out of the ring.

Question-and-answer drives home many points, whether the
pupil or the teacher is the questioner. Questions from pupil to teacher show real interest.

The following is a cross-section of questions from actual class
work:

Q.: Are most horses "easy" at the jog?

A.: No, some of them have a very rough jog. Easiness of gait is re-
lated to length of the horse's pastern, and relaxed body.

* * * *

Q.: Will you give the aids for the jog?

A.: Slight pressure from both legs at No. 1 position.

Q.: For the lope?

A.: Outside leg at No. 2 position; inside leg at No. 1. Inside leg says; "Take canter". Outside leg tells the horse which lead to take.

* * * *

Q.: Please give the aids for straightening a horse that is backing crookedly.

A.: If he is going off to the left, use the left leg at No. 2. Use the rein aids for the back; use the legs to correct the direction.

* * * *

Q.: Why do you have us circle so often?

A.: Circling increases the rider's control of the horse and helps build up the rider's confidence because he is controlling the horse.

Q.: Why do you work us to the right so much?

A.: Because in general horses and riders execute a circle to the left better than to the right. Therefore, to develop equal skill, I have you go more frequently to the right. However, I do not want to overdo this. Working too often in either direction makes the horses "one-sided".

* * * *

Q.: If it is incorrect for us to look down at the horse's shoulder, how do we know which lead he is going to take?

A.: Keep your eyes up to see where you are going. With practice, you will develop the ability to "feel" which lead the horse is going to take. You will feel it while he is still in the walk or trot — feel it through your leg or seat.

* * * *

Q.: When a horse is on the wrong lead, how do you correct him?

A.: Bring him back to the jog and take the lope again, giving the correct aids, which are: Outside leg at No. 2; inside leg at No. 1; slight raise of inside rein. Be sure the horse understands which lead is required.

* * * *

Q.: In riding flat saddle, for Eastern shows and for hunts, does a rider have to use change of leads?

A.: Yes. Eastern riders have change in direction just as you do.

* * * *

Q.: What are the disadvantages encountered when a horse is dis-united?

A.: At best, there's a loss of efficiency. At worst, he may fall, besides, a disunited horse is awkward.

* * * *

Q.: What are the disadvantages of a horse loping on a wrong lead?

A.: You might take a spill, because the horse, when turning, is apt to cross his front legs.

* * * *

Q.: How would you define the importance of leads?

101

A.: A horse on the correct lead is maintaining balance. Balance is imperative in movement.

Q.: Shall we practice our position and aids at home?

A.: Yes. Be sure you are correct, however. Remember, I can tell them to you and we can school here. But YOU are the only one who can get YOU to do something.

* * * *

Q.: Horses and colts in the pasture run and sometimes run in loops. Do they change leads correctly?

A.: Yes. They do. Their own natural sense of balance is very great.

Q.: Then why does a rider have to give aids and watch to see that a horse is going into the correct lead? Why not just trust to him to do it naturally?

A.: Because the addition of a rider's weight has given the horse a new problem in balance. Nature teaches him to balance his own weight, but, when 150 pounds or more of rider are added, usually he has to learn all over again.

* * * *

Q.: In making a figure 8, where is the proper place for change of leads?

A.: At the intersection of the two circles, when the horse changes direction.

Q.: Sometimes a horse almost stumbles at this point. Other times he gives just a little skip. Can he do it without any skip at all?

A.: Yes, indeed. The correct change of leads, made with all four feet off the ground, is entirely smooth.

Q.: Why should neck reining be done as near the withers as the saddle horn will allow?

A.: Neck reining too high toward the horse's ears leads to the horse turning with more weight than is proper on the forehand, or flipping the hindquarters. The forehand is not constructed to handle the weight, and reining low tends to keep horse's neck in line with his body and assists in moving forehand more lightly.

* * * *

Q.: Why is one hand free in Western riding?

A.: The Westerner wants his right hand free to handle his rope; in early days, to be prepared to handle his gun. Hence, the reins in the left hand.

Q.: Why is that rider over there using the right hand on the reins?

A.: That rider is left-handed.

Q.: Would this be explained to a judge in a show?

A.: No. Unfortunately, some judges forget to take this into consideration.

Q.: What does it mean when someone says a horse has a "rubber mouth?"

A.: A rubber-mouthed horse is a horse that protects his mouth by clamping his jaw. When the rider reins back, all he gets is an action as if the horse's neck was made of rubber. This is a difficult type of mouth to cope with. The best thing to do is to treat the animal as if he has never been bridled before and attempt to re-mouth him.

An alternative, which may apply to a hard-mouthed horse, is for the rider to seek a substitute for the rein aids. This may be a hackamore. Any other substitute aid would have to be legs, weight or voice.

You will learn about care of the horse's mouth, and proper bits and bitting, in the advanced class.

PART III

ADVANCED

Chapter VII

AN ADVANCED CLASS

It is assumed that, at the conclusion of their intermediate training, the riders in your class have thorough, routined knowledge of:

> their leads;
> the use and application of the aids;

and that they can:

> maintain correct position;
> do the limbering up exercises at all gaits;
> ride and show a *schooled* horse.

At the conclusion of the advanced course, students should be able to teach beginners; school a horse; train another rider in schooling; and give a creditable performance in a standard AHSA or AQHA horse show.

They should also have a working knowledge of judging and the obligations entailed.

Besides holding regular classes, in which students not only continue work on their own horsemanship but learn to school their horses, it is well to let individual riders take over the class for part of a session. The ones who prove especially talented in this direction can be invited to be guest instructors at a beginners' class — with you standing by as an observer, however. Training of beginners is so important that the instruction of student-teachers needs close supervision.

Nothing in your whole course is more vital to the future of horsemanship than turning some of your pupils into good teachers. Ability in this direction is precious and should be given every chance to grow and function.

Judging ability can be developed in advanced students by requiring them, one by one, to judge their classmates. Also, when local horse shows are held, your class will certainly attend and the members will enter many events. When not riding, the members of your class can sit together and try judging the different events, comparing their scoring with that of the professional judges.

A discussion period on this scoring can be held afterward during part of a lesson session.

If a student has a flair for judging, he is well worth encouraging. Able, well-grounded judges are badly needed, and a popular and respected judge can add most interesting and broadening experience to his career as a horseman.

There are Judges Clinics held by the D.G.W.S.; the Arab Association; Walking Horse Association; and other organizations; Dates for such clinics can be obtained from these breeders associations, and you would be wise to urge your budding judges to attend them.

You, as teacher, should point out that it takes a combination of qualities to be a good judge — among them, *besides* devotion to and knowledge of horses, an alert and unflagging ability to see and evaluate quickly; the physical stamina to stand for long hours in a dusty arena; the self-confidence to make and abide by a decision; the ability to judge a horse and rider objectively, strictly on present performance; and the tact and patience to soothe a disappointed or disgruntled contestant and try to make him learn from his failure. A judge must be honest with himself and the exhibitor, but he must also be the "diplomat" in the horse world.

The greater number of your advanced riders, of course, will show rather than judge. And, also, you want them to come home from the shows of the vicinity fluttering with ribbons and carrying a goodly assortment of trophies.

The more time they can devote to well worked out practice routines, the better their chances.

One kind of training, which is excellent in general and which prepares your riders for an event that is growing more and more popular, is for the arena tests. Arena tests are a series of logical training movements, combined into patterns, and they will be discussed in detail in a forthcoming chapter.

Now, as to the schooling of the horse. Always, in such training, it should be remembered that the Western horse is a working horse. He shows, yes. More and more each year. But his skills are functional. They can be used, to the profit of the owner, on the ranch as well as in the show ring.

Chapter IV on Movements incorporates general suggestions for training a horse in the eight basic movements, outlining faults to be avoided, as well as procedure to follow.

One feature of horsemanship the importance of which cannot be too much emphasized and which you would do well to take up thoroughly with your advanced students is summed up in the next chapter, Bits and Bitting.

Chapter VIII

BITS AND BITTING

The bitting of a horse could be termed an art. Thousands of bits, of endless variety, have been used since the horse was first bitted by man.

If it were possible to study the mouth of each horse, we could readily see why, ideally, every horse should have a different bit. No two horses have the same mouth, and not only is the mouth different but the reaction and degree of sensitivity of each horse is different. And each rider who mounts a horse has a different type of hand that feels different to the horse. Here again, ideally, the horse needs a different bit for every rider.

However, since we cannot have this infinity of bits, we must do the best we can with what we have. A rider should endeavor to find which bit best suits his own horse. He should not expect a bit to be successful because it is one his neighbor's horse goes exceptionally well in.

There are three general type of bits:

The bar bit, (Ill. 46a) which has solid mouth-piece without a shank or leverage action. In this bit a minimum of pressure is put on the bars of the horse's mouth (that is, the area between molars and incisors) and a maximum on his tongue. This is the lightest form of bit.

The snaffle bit, (Ill. 46b) with a jointed mouth-piece. This is the oldest, most generally used and satisfactory of all forms of bits ever devised.

The curb bit, (Ill. 47) in which lever action is obtained to increase the amount of pressure on the bars of the horse's mouth. Curb bits include the spade bit, grazing bit, half-breed bit — any bit without snaffle attachments, with a shank and curb strap or chain for leverage. There are thousands of different sizes, shapes, and forms of mouth-pieces.

A common misnomer is calling the light training curb bit with the broken mouth piece of a snaffle. (Ill. 47f) It also falls in the curb family.

The first two types of bit, the bar bit and the snaffle, are mild bits.

A bar bit, which is more generally used for driving than for riding, has a straight or very slightly curved mouth-piece, with a medium sized ring at either end. With the addition of the shank, it is commonly called a "Pelham". (Ill. 47d) If this Pelham is used without a curb strap, it is even milder, since part of the pressure is transferred to the cheek straps and from there to the top of the head, or poll.

The snaffle bit is the mildest of the riding bits. This should be

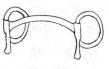

1A   BAR BIT

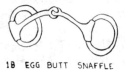

1B EGG BUTT SNAFFLE

1C MOUTHING SNAFFLE

ILL. 46 SNAFFLE BITS

the first used on a young horse. The action of the mouthpiece is on both the tongue and bars and should act on the same part of the mouth as it does with the curb bit. The horse then begins to acquire a feeling of what is to come when he is ridden with a curb bit. The thicker the bit at the extremes, the milder it is. A snaffle bit has no lever action, with the result that the power applied on the reins is conveyed unincreased to the mouth of the horse. There is, however, a slight pressure action on the bars. There are many kinds of mouth-pieces in the snaffle bits, including the mouthing bit (Ill. 46c) and the double-jointed mouth-piece.

The curb bit has as many different shapes and forms as the snaffle and, contrary to the general concept, it is not just a Western bit. Introduced to America by the Spaniards, it was used as early as the fourteenth century in Europe. (Ill. 47a)

The mouthpiece of the curb bit may range from straight bar to a slight curve; from a low port to the high port of the spade bit. (Ill. 47b) The upper branches are always straight or bent out slightly so as not to interfere with the horse's cheek. The lower branches may be straight, single or double curved. The Chifney or Whitman bit (Ill. 47c) has double upper branches, one for the attachment of the cheek pieces, the other for the curb strap. This type of curb bit takes all pressure off the top of the horse's head.

The end and aim of all bitting is to have the slightest wish of the rider obeyed by the horse without constraint, resistance, or exhibition of temper. It is only through knowledge of bitting that perfect control of the horse can be obtained. To do this without the infliction of unnecessary pain is vital to the steadiness of the horse.

The horse's head is the lever by which command over the neck is gained.

Lever action from the reins is greatest when the horse's head is at right angle to his neck. The more the head departs from that

110

position, due to severe bitting or other cause, the more difficult is the lever action. If the horse's head is brought in until it touches his chest, there is no lever action at all, resulting in evasion of bit control.

The rider should regard the bit as a means of communication, as well as a check to "master" the animal. The horse's awareness of the bit varies from the slightest of sensations to the most intense pain. If the intensity of the effect of the bit does not accord with the sensitivity and intelligence of the horse, it may provoke rebellion or resistance.

On the other hand, when the effects of the bit are suited to the sensitiveness of the horse's mouth, his intelligence and training, the bit becomes the rational and useful instrument it is intended to be.

In selecting a bit for a particular horse, there are many factors to consider — his age, his temperament, his degree of training, and the type of work he is to perform. The snaffle and hackamore are most frequently used on young or green horses. The latter is often necessary for a horse whose mouth is ruined or spoiled. The Western curb with snaffle mouth-piece is often seen on the "grade school" or intermediate horse and even on the finished horse; the grazing bit on the ranch horse; the spade on the highly schooled stock horse of the far West; the plain curb of low port on the every-day pleasure horse.

After the general type of bit has been chosen, there is the matter of fitting.

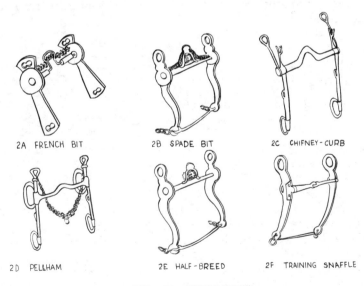

| 2A FRENCH BIT | 2B SPADE BIT | 2C CHIFNEY-CURB |
| 2D PELLHAM | 2E HALF-BREED | 2F TRAINING SNAFFLE |

ILL. 47 CURB BITS

The bit in the horse's mouth should fit so that there is a slight wrinkling of his lips. Adjust the bit, however, up or down so that it will hit no teeth. (Ill. 48)

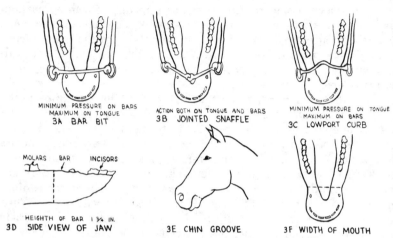

ILL. 48   BIT ACTION

To check the tightness of the curb chain, insert two fingers between the jaw and the curb chain, take hold of both reins, pull back, and, from the straight line or normal drop the shank should be about thirty to forty degrees. (Ill. 49c)

In the fitting of any bit, the shape of the horse's mouth must be considered.

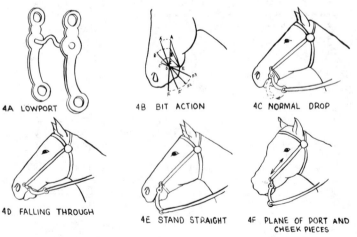

ILL. 49   CURB BIT ACTION (SIDE)

A horse's two jaw bones unite just above the lower lip to form what is called the chin groove. (Ill. 48e) It is here that the chin strap should sit, since considerable pressure can be applied in this area without causing undue pain.

Immediately above this chin groove, the nature of the bone and skin changes. The bone has sharp edges and the skin is very thin and sensitive. These sharp edges should be especially considered. Too often these bones are chipped or broken by an illfitting bit, causing calcification and "callouses".

The horse's tongue lies in a groove or channel.

Between the incisors and molars is an area devoid of teeth except for the tusks. This area is called *the bars*, and it is here that the mouth-piece of the bit lies. (Ill. 48d)

The bars must be carefully examined, for it is upon these sensitive gums that the action of the bit takes place.

There is general uniformity in the height of the bars but great diversity in their shape. The height of the bars has been found to be rather consistant at some $1\frac{3}{4}$ inches. (Ill. 48d)

The width of the horse's mouth, measured at the height of the chin groove, varies from $3\frac{1}{2}$ to $5\frac{1}{2}$ inches. (Ill. 48f)

The tongue channel, or distance between the bars, generally measures about $1\frac{1}{3}$ inches.

The cheek pieces should clear the sides of the mouth. Since the height of the bars is usually $1\frac{3}{4}$ inches, this gives a total length of the upper cheek piece of about $3\frac{3}{4}$ inches. This is important because the dimensions of the curb bit are proportional to it.

The port should be the width of the tongue channel. Even if the mouth-piece has the proper width, if the port is wider than the tongue channel, one or both of the corners of the port will bear on the bars, causing pain for no purpose. When the tongue lies in its channel, it helps support the bit and receives the first action of reining. Bear in mind that the tongue is a very delicate organ and that no horse is more useless than one with a cut tongue.

The curb bits are the only ones with lever action, where the power on the reins is mechanically increased before it reaches the horse's mouth.

There are several types of lever action, and whether such action is favorable or not depends on the arrangement of the bit and curb chain.

In one type of leverage, the power is applied at one end. the weight at the other, with the fulcrum between the two; the power and weight move around the fulcrum in opposite directions.

In another type, the power and fulcrum are at opposite extremities of the lever, the weight between the two. The power and weight move in the same direction, rotating around the fulcrum.

In the first leverage, let us say the power is in the reins, the horse's bars are the fulcrum, and the curb chain is the weight. The effect will be understandable. The stronger the pull, the more the horse will stick his nose out.

In the lever of the second type, on the other hand, the power is applied through the reins, the tightened curb chain is the fulcrum, the weight the pressure on the bars. This will cause the horse's head to move correctly, following the direction of the rider's hands.

Curb bits should be adjusted so as to get sufficient power on the horse's bars without causing an unnecessary degree of pain. Thus, bits not too large in dimension are reliable in their action and insure efficiency with a minimum of discomfort to the horse.

In curb bits, the important points to be determined are the length of cheek pieces and the proportion of the upper and lower branches. The height of the bars is $1\frac{3}{4}$ inches from the center of the mouth-piece to the height of the curb strap attachments, or the lowest point of the ring. The lower branch of the cheek piece, measured from the center of the lower ring, is twice as long as the $1\frac{3}{4}$ inches, or $3\frac{1}{2}$ inches.

Good bitting neither allows a bit to "fall through" nor to "stand straight", the latter meaning a bit with the curb strap so tight that there is no play, causing a horse to poke his nose out instead of following the rider's hands.

The length of the upper branch of the cheek piece will cause this instrument either to stand stiff or fall through, if it exceeds, or is shorter than, the height of the bars.

In Fig. Ill. 49b, D-E represents the height of the bars, D-B an upper branch equal to D-E, D-C one of only half the same lengths, and D-A one double the length. When a pull of the rein acts at F on the lower branch, the curb will be drawn closer to the horse's chin, and the mouthpiece back against the bars. If the amount of this closing up is equal in all three instances, the bit with a long upper branch D-A will assume the position A^1-D-F^1. It will be stiff and the curb acting upward in the direction E-A^1 will press on the sensitive part of the horse's jaw. There will be no lever action, the two arms of the lever being equal, and the horse will bore into the rider's hands.

Or, if the short upper branch D-C equals half D-E, it will assume the position C^1-D-F^3, that is, it will fall through, and the curb chain or strap will remain in the chin groove and act forward in the direction E-C^1. However, forming a very acute angle with the branches of the bit, it will have scarcely any value as a fulcrum. The lever action, in this instance, will be very great; in fact, too great.

Now, let the intermediate upper branch D-B, equal to D-E, assume the position B^1-D-F^2. It will neither be stiff nor fall through. The curb will remain in the chin groove, acting obliquely, and, since the lower branch of the lever F-D is in proportion of 2 to 1 to the upper one D-B, there will be the proportion of 2 to 1 to the upper one D-B, there will be the proper lever action.

The angle at which the reins act on the bit is important, and the action is better when the power is applied at a right angle. (See 49) Having computed the height of the bars and the length of the upper branches of the bit, if the lower branches are double this height, one gets about 5¼ inches overall, which is ample leverage for the average horse.

What should be the position of the curb strap in relation to the bit in the horse's mouth? Remember that when the curb strap lies in the chin groove, it is a painless fulcrum, but if it rides up on the sharp bones of the lower jaw it causes undue pain, rendering the best constructed bit uncertain in action. When the bit is properly placed, the mouth-piece is an nearly opposite the chin groove as the tusks will allow.

The curb chain or strap must also be fitted properly, with the fact borne in mind that leather is prone to stretch or shrink. If the curb chain or strap is too wide, it will ride upon the sharp cheek bones; if too narrow, it will cause too much pain.

Hard and fast figures as to the exact length of a strap are not possible, but, exclusive of curb hooks, it should be about more than the width of the mouth, or 1½ times the length of the mouth-piece, if it is of leather.

No part of the curb bit is more important than the mouth-piece due to its immediate pressure on the mouth. If the mouth-piece is too wide, the curb chain or strap will bear more or less on a particular spot and cause a sore in the chin groove. The mouth-piece should be exactly the same width as the width of the mouth; thus, the curb chain will wrap closely around the chin, pressing equally over a large surface.

The form and proportions of the mouth-piece must conform to the size of the horse's tongue and bars. The fleshy tongue is less sensitive to pressure than the bony bars. If a straight, unjointed mouth-piece of moderate thickness is used, this, resting wholly on the animal's tongue, would be the lightest form of curb bit, notwithstanding the lever action.

However, with the use of a port or upward curve in the mouth-piece, pressure is removed from the tongue and transferred to the sensitive bars, and, with only the same lever action as before, the severest form of curb bit results.

Between these two extremes there is a wide range of bitting, and the whole art consists, as far as the mouth-piece is concerned, in determining how much pressure should fall on the horse's tongue and how much on his bars.

The height of the port is the most variable dimension of all.

It depends on the thickness of the horse's tongue and sensitivity of his bars, the temperament and conformation of the animal, and the service to which he is to be put.

The most severe bit that should ever be necessary is one where the height of the port is equal to its width, or about $1\frac{1}{3}$ inches. Any higher port would strike the palate, causing unnecessary pain and inducing the horse to bore with his head away from the rider's hand.

The plane of the port should coincide with the plane of the check pieces, if they are straight. (Ill. 49f) If they are curved, then the plane of the port should coincide with the plane of the upper branches. The use of the ring for upper branches helps relieve the rein-pull conveyed to the horse's poll. It has been found that a shorter upper branch has a tendency to fall through and pinch the horse's mouth.

No horse has a naturally "hard" mouth. The condition thus described comes about in many ways, for instance:

(1) A particular horse may not have the physical coordination for quick response.

(2) A very sensitive-mouthed horse will defend his mouth with a tight jaw and rigid poll.

(3) A horse may have his bars injured by breaking or chipping of the bony area or there may be an injury to the nerve.

(4) A horse may be so mentally disturbed or high strung that his mental attitude tends to rule over bit obedience.

A horse with a cut tongue will fall in to category (3), or a horse that has learned to curl his tongue away from the bit. The curling of the tongue may begin through improper bitting of a young animal, or it may come from unyielding hands of the rider, from which the tongue tends to seek relief by evading the bit.

The teacher should never stop stressing the importance of hands. No amount of proper bitting will protect a horse from rough hands. An ordinarily conscientious rider, in one unthinking moment, can ruin a horse's mouth by a jerk on the reins. It takes only one such action, with its lamentable result, to bring home to a rider how precious and irreplaceable is his horse's mouth.

Things to be Remembered about Bitting:

Bits should be made of the best and lightest material possible.

* * *

The correct application of the snaffle bit to a colt's mouth leads to future usefulness of the animal as a mature horse.

* * *

A horse should be governed, not by pain, but by his knowledge and understanding of the principles of reward and punishment.

* * *

Never change a bit with the idea of making the horse obedient by the infliction of pain. A bit is strictly for control. The whip, voice, and spur are the only legitimate instrument of punishment.

* * *

Meet obedience with kindness, misconduct with punishment.

* * *

Absence of stiffness, constraint, or painful action are the characteristics of good bitting.

* * *

Some horses require a greater length in the bit's shank, but a heavy bit will not stop a confirmed bolter. On other hand, a mild bit will often accomplish everything a severe bit will not.

* * *

A young horse, new to the saddle, may give the impression of "hard" mouth when really his mouth is sensitive. The equilibrium of the horse is disturbed by the rider's weight, and the horse, seeking a fifth leg, may bore on the bit. When the horse has learned to carry the rider, he no longer seeks this support and his mouth gives the feel of being more tender.

* * *

Even with rational bits, good results can only be obtained through the constant exercise of judgement, patience and care by the rider — and by the rider's light, steady and educated hands.

Chapter IX

ARENA TESTS

There is an ever-increasing demand in today's western training groups and horse shows for a type of progressive tests known as arena tests.

These are a series of logical training movements, combined at first into easy patterns, then becoming increasingly more advanced. These tests are designed to measure the schooling of a horse and the ability, tact and understanding of the rider.

The tests should start with the young or green horse and novice rider, and in successive degrees be carried on until they show the qualities required in a finished horse and finished rider: complete tractibility on the part of the horse, but with the freedom of action and animation of a horse at liberty; tact and polish on the part of the rider revealed by his ability to obtain any of the required gaits and movements from the horse without observable use of aids.

GOALS FOR EACH TEST

In the different tests, a horse should be able to:

Test 1, have good walk, jog, lope; halt squarely from the walk and stand quietly; execute the large circle at the walk, jog and lope; halt and walk off. 90° off-set at walk and jog.

Tests 2, and in addition to the above, do a 180° rollback on the hindquarters at walk, jog; halt from walk and jog; back and walk off; take small circle at walk, jog; show simple change of leads in large circle at lope; serpentine at walk and jog; trot out; gallop out.

Tests 3, In addition to the above, do a 180° turn on hindquarters at lope; halt from lope; halt and lope off; back, jog off; small circle at lope; serpentine at lope with simple change of leads; 360 degree pivot at walk; two track at the walk.

Test 4, Back and lope off; serpentine, flying change at lope; 360° degree turn at walk and jog; offset, i.e. 180 degree turn twice; two track at jog; inside spin on a circle.

Test 5, Show flying change of leads; rollback; halt; offset; spin; do figure eights; 360 degree pivot at lope; offset three times; two track at lope; two to three inside spins on a circle at the lope. In this test, the horse should be able to do all of these movements at any speed.

ARENA TEST I-A

Marks		Time allowed—8 minutes		
10-9	Very Good	Time penalties—1 point for	1st time	1 point
8-7	Good	every 10 seconds over time	2nd time	3 points
6-5	Sufficient	allowed or fraction there-	3rd time	6 points
4-3	Insufficient	of. To be ridden in plain	4th time	Elimination
2-1	Poor	snaffle, one hand light	Leaving	
0	Not Performed	grazing bit or simple	Arena	Elimination
		double bridle.	Error	Penalties

To be ridden in a plain snaffle, hackamore or light grazing bit (the later may be up to the show management). Two hands may be used.

Contestant's Name		Contestant's Number	

	Movements	Score 0-10	Comments
1 A	Enter ordinary walk		
X	Halt. Acknowledge Judge. Proceed at ordinary walk		
C	Track to right		
2 A	Jog		
K-M	Cross diagonal		
C	Halt (5 seconds), continue jog		
H-F	Cross diagonal, extend trot		
3 F-A	Jog		
A	Ordinary walk		
E	Halt. Turn on hindquarters 180° (roll back) to right Resume ordinary walk		
5 C	Circle, tangent to sides, developing ordinary lope, right lead. On approaching C second time track to right at jog		
6 M-X-K	Cross diagonal. Halt X. Resume jog		
7 A	Circle, tangent to sides, developing ordinary lope, left lead. On approaching A second time, track to left, jog		
8 A-C	Serpentine, width of ring of five loops		
C	Track to right, ordinary jog, walk at M.		
9 M-X-K	Cross diagonal, strong walk		
A	Go up center line		
X	Halt. Acknowledge Judge. Leave arena track to right on loose rein, free walk.		
10	GENERAL IMPRESSION Impulsion Ease and freedom of gaits.		

11	Suppleness and lightness of horse in movements.		
12	Position and seat of rider. Correct use of aids.		
	Total		
	Penalties		
	Final Score		

Judge's Signature

ARENA TEST 2-A

Marks		Time allowed—8 minutes	Error	Penalties
10-9	Very Good	Time penalties—1 point for	1st time	1 point
8-7	Good	every 10 seconds over time	2nd time	3 points
6-5	Sufficient	allowed or fraction there-	3rd time	6 points
4-3	Insufficient	of. To be ridden in plain	4th time	Elimination
2-1	Poor	snaffle, with light grazing		
0	Not Performed	bit or simple double bridle.	Arena	Elimination

Contestant's Name		Contestant's Number

	Movements	Score 0-10	Comments
1 A	Enter jog		
X	Halt. Ackowledge Judge. Proceed ordinary walk.		
C	Track right		
2 B-A	Jog		
A	Small circle (20' diameter)		
3 K-X-M	Cross diagonal		
C	Halt. Back 6 steps Proceed ordinary walk		
4 E-A	Jog		
A	Small Circle		
F-X-H	Cross diagonal		
5 C-A	Serpentine of 4 loops (16' 6") diameter each side of center line (6 loops for large arena)		
A	Track left, ordinary canter.		
6 A-B-C-E	Ordinary canter, left lead		
E	Small Circle		

7	K	Half circle. Without change of leads return to track at E
	E	Simple change of lead, right.
8	B	Small circle
	F	Half circle. Without change of lead return to track at B
	B	Simple change of lead, left
9	H-K	Strong lope
	K-F	Ordinary lope
	F-X-H	Cross diagonal, simple change at H.
10	M-F	Strong lope
	F-A	Ordinary lope
11	A	Jog
	K-X-M	Cross diagonal, strong trot
	C-M	Jog
12	C	Check, turn on haunches 180° (roll back), left resume jog
13	M-F	Strong trot
	F-A	Jog
14	K	Check, turn on haunches 180° (roll back) right, resume ordinary jog
15	A	Down center line, left
	X	Halt. Ackowledge Judge Leave ring at free walk, track right.
16		GENERAL IMPRESSIONS Impulsion and quality of gaits
17		Suppleness, lightness and obedience in execution of movements
18		Position and seat of rider. Correct use of aids.
		Total
		Penalties
		Final Score

Judge's Signature

ARENA TEST 3

Marks				
10-9	Very Good	Time allowed—8 minutes	1st time	1 point
8-7	Good	Time penalties—1 point for	2nd time	3 points
6-5	Sufficient	every 10 seconds over time	3rd time	6 points
4-3	Insufficient	allowed or fraction there-	4th time	Elimination
2-1	Poor	of. To be ridden in plain	Leaving	
0-	Not Performed	snaffle, with light grazing	Arena	Elimination
		bit or simple double bridle.	Error	Penalties

Contestant's Name

Contestant's Number

	Movements	Score 0-10	Comments
1 A	Enter Lope		
X	Halt, Ackowledge Judge		
2 X-C-B	Jog		
A	Halt, (5 seconds) Proceed at jog		
K-X-H	Pass, jog, track right		
3 M-X-F	Pass (two track)		
F-A-D	Up center line at jog		
D	Spin right, once continue jog		
G	Spin left, once continue jog to C		
4 C	Lope, track left		
E	Small circle left		
K	Half circle		
E	Flying change of leads		
5 B	Small circle right		
F	Half circle		
B	Flying change of leads		
6 H-K	Gallop		
K	Lope		
A	Up center line		
7 G	Roll back right, gallop		
A	Take track right at lope		
K-H	Gallop		
8 H-C	Lope		
C	Go down center line		
D	Roll back left. Gallop		
G	Halt, back 6 steps, take lope right lead		

9	B	Right turn, with X as center
	X	Make 1 large figure eight at gallop, first circle right 66′ diameter
	X	Halt. Immobile 5 seconds.
10	X	Then take lope left lead. Circle to left where circle intersects center line, perform inside spin. Make one more circle.
	X	Change leads. Take track right. Circle to right. Where circle intersects center line perform inside spin right, then one more circle to right.
11	X	Walk
	E	Track to right
	C	Jog
	M-X-K	Long trot, loose rein
12	K	Jog (ordinary)
	A	Halt. Back 10 steps. Proceed at jog
	F-X-H	Long trot, loose rein
13	H	Jog (ordinary)
	C	Lope right lead
	A	Up center line
	G	Halt. Acknowledge Judge
		Leave arena on loose rein
14		GENERAL IMPRESSIONS Impulsion and quality of gaits
15		Suppleness, lightness and obedience in execution of movements
16		Position and seat of rider Correct use of aids

Total
Penalties
Final Score

Judge's Signature

Diagram for Competition
Movement 10 in Arena Test 3 Ill. 50

Take lope left lead. Circle to left; where circle intersects line, perform inside spin to left. Make one more circle to left. Repeat to right.

ARENA TEST 4

Marks		Time allowed—8 minutes	1st time	1 point
10-9	Very Good	Time penalties—1 point for	2nd time	3 points
8-7	Good	every 10 seconds over time	3rd time	6 points
6-5	Sufficient	allowed or fraction there-	4th time	Elimination
4-3	Insufficient	of. To be ridden in plain	Leaving	
2-1	Poor	snaffle, with light grazing	Arena	Elimination
0	Not Performed	bit or simple double bridle.	Error Penalties	

Contestant's   Contestant's
Name   Number

		Movements	Score 0-10	Comments
1	A	Enter at lope		
	X	Halt salute judge, Jog		
	C	Track right. cross diagonals		
	M-X-K	Extended trot		
2	K	Jog		
	A	Lope		
	B	Turn left		
	X	Circle left 66' diameter on returning to X		
3	X	Change lead. circle right 66' diameter		
4	X	Upon returning to X change to left lead, make circle 20' in diameter		
	X	Change to right lead and make circle 20' in diameter. upon returning to X, Jog		
5	E	Track right		
	H	Lope		
	C	Turn down center line		
	G-D	Gallop. roll back left at D		
6	X	Halt. Back 6 steps. Gallop left lead		
	G	Roll back right		
	X	Halt. Back 6 steps. Gallop right lead		
7	D	Roll back right		
	X	Spin right 360 degrees coming out on right lead, continue to G		
	G	Roll back left		
8	X	Spin 360 degrees left coming out on left lead, continue to D		
	D	Halt. stand immoble 5 seconds		

9	D	Lope right lead
	E	Turn right
	X	Circle right 66' diameter, upon returning to
	X	Change leads and circle left 66' diameter

10	X	Change leads and circle right 20' diameter
	X	Change leads and circle left 20' diameter
	X	Halt

11	X	Jog, track left
	H-F	Strong trot, loose rein

12	F	Jog
	A	Up center line
	X	Halt, salute, leave ring at a walk on loose rein.

13	GENERAL IMPRESSIONS Impulsion and quality of gaits

14	Suppleness, lightness and obedience in execution of movements

15	Position and seat of rider. Correct use of aids.

Total
Penalties
Final Score

Judge's Signature

ARENA TEST 5

Marks		Time allowed—8 minutes	1st time	1 point
10-9	Very Good	Time penalties—1 point for	2nd time	3 points
8-7	Good	every 10 seconds over time	3rd time	6 points
6-5	Sufficient	allowed or fraction there-	4th time	Elimination
4-3	Insufficient	of. To be ridden in plain	Leaving	
2-1	Poor	snaffle, with light grazing	Arena	Elimination
0	Not Performed	bit or simple double bridle.	Error	Penalties

	Movements	Score 0-10	Comments

		Movements	Score 0-10	Comments
1	A	Enter jog		
	X	Halt salute		
2	X	Lope left lead		
	C	Track left		
	E	Small circle left 20′ in diameter		
3	K	Jog		
	A	Turn up center line		
	X	Halt, Take right lead, track right at C		
	B	Small circle right, 20′		
4	B	Upon returning to B enlarge circle to 66′		
	R	Spin right when circle crosses center line		
	L	Roll back left.		
5	R	Spin left		
	L	Roll back right		
	B	Jog, continue track right		
6	K-X-M	Extended trot		
	M	Jog		
	H-X-F	Extended trot		
	F	Jog		
7	F-A	Lope, up center line		
	D-G	Gallop		
	G	Halt. Back 10 steps. Lope		
8	C	Track left		
	A	Serpentine 5 loops, changing leads at center line. Track left at C.		
	H-X-F	Change lead at X		
9	X-A	Up center line		
	X	Halt. Spin once left. Spin once right.		
10	X	Loose reins, walk to		
	G	Halt salute, leave on loose rein.		
11		GENERAL IMPRESSION Impulsion and quality of gaits		

126

| 12 | Suppleness, lightness and obedience in execution of movements |
| 13 | Position and seat of rider Correct use of aids |

Total
Penalties
Final Score

Judge's Signature

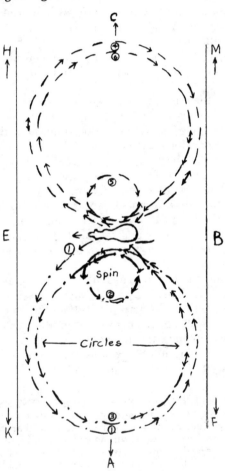

Movement 10 in Arena Test—3
Take lope left ahead. Circle to left; where circle intersects line,
perform inside spin to left. Make one more circle to left. Repeat to R.

ILL. 50

Chapter X
SHOWS AND SHOWING
(MISCELLANEOUS CLASSES)

Showing is regarded by individual horseman in different ways — as a highly skilled art, a profession, a competitive hobby, or as a pastime.

This chapter will discuss at length the events that intermediate and advanced students of Western riding may aspire to enter and in which they should achieve a creditable showing. The events in Chapter XI are for advanced riders.

The rules quoted are from the official handbooks of the American Quarter Horse Association and the American Horse Show Association, with permission being granted by A.Q.H.A. and A.H.S.A. for this publication. They are given considerable space here so that these chapters can be used as reference by the reader, teacher or students.

Remember, they are subject to yearly change.

There are at present two types of shows, those under the rules of the American Horse Shows Association and those under the American Quarter Horse Association. The gap between the rules and requirements of the two is not as great as it was ten years ago. The time should not be far off when they will honor each other. (This occurred in 1965). Essentially, the two associations seek the same thing in the working horse. Any apparent difference between the two has been due to lack of understanding on the part of each as to the aims and purposes and terminology of the other. In regard to terminology, for instance, the *reining* horse of AQHA is the same as the *stock* horse of AHSA.

As far as showing is concerned, the following pages list all the classes. In the AQHA listing are Western Pleasure, Working Cow Horse, Western Riding, Western Trail, Pole Bending, Barrel Racing, Roping, Reining, Cutting, Racing and Jumping; also the new Youth Activities, which include the foregoing as well as Breakaway Roping, Showing at Halter, and Showmanship.

In the Pleasure Classes, the rules read:

AQHA

WESTERN PLEASURE HORSE CONTEST
(This class receives half points.)

No horse shall be allowed to show in more than one approved AQHA registered western pleasure class per show.

Horses are to be shown at a walk, trot and lope on a reasonably loose rein without undue restraint. Horses must work both ways of the ring at all three gaits to demonstrate their ability with different leads. The judge shall have the right to ask for additional work from any horse.

Horses are to be reversed to the inside (away from the rail). Horses may be required to reverse at any gait, or may be required to go from any gait to any other gait, at the discretion of the judge.

Entries shall be penalized for being on wrong leads. excessive speed is to be penalized.

Appointments: Horses shall be shown with a stock saddle, but silver equipment will not count over a good working outfit. A hackamore or a curb, half-breed or spade bit is permissible but a martingale or tiedown is prohibited. No wire curbs, regardless of how padded or taped, or no chin strap narrower than one-half inch will be permitted. Chain curbs are permissible but must be of the standard flat variety with no twist and must meet the approval of the judge.

Riders shall wear western hat and cowboy boots. The use of spurs, chaps or similar gear, and the carrying of a rope or riata is optional.

This class will be judged on the performance and conformation of the horse at the discretion of the judge.

The use of shoes other than standard horseshoes (or extended hooves) is to be discouraged and may be penalized by the judge.

Reins shall be held in one hand and cannot be changed during performance. The free hand shall not be used to support the rider by being placed on any part of the saddle.

AHSA

WESTERN PLEASURE HORSES

Part. I General

Sec. 1. Horses shall be of any breed or combination of breeds 14.1 hands and over, serviceably sound, in good condition and of stock horse type. A full mane is not required. Entries may be judged for soundness and conformation before entering the arena. The use of shoes other than standard horse shoes is to be discouraged and may be penalized by the Judge.

Sec. 2. Appointments.

(a) Personal. Riders shall wear Western hat, chaps, shotgun chaps or chinks, cowboy boots and carry a rope or reata. Spurs are optional. A rain slicker may be required in Trail and Pleasure classes provided it is so stipulated in the prize list.

(b) Trail and Pleasure Horse Classes. Entries shall be shown with a stock saddle, but silver equipment will not count over a good working outfit. There shall be no discrimination against any type of Western bit but no hackamore, hackamore bit or other device except a standard Western bit shall be allowed. A curb, half-breed or spade bit is permissible but a bosal or cavesson-type noseband, martigale or tie-down is prohibited. No wire, chain or other metal or rawhide device may be used in conjuction with, or as part of, the leather chin strap. If split reins are used and horse is broken to ground tying, no hobbles are necessary but if closed reins are used and a horse is hobble broken, hobbles must be carried.

The main difference between the two here is that the AQHA rules apply to the quarter horse breed, whereas the AHSA class is open to any breed used as a western *pleasure* horse. Also, there are no appointments and conformation is at the option of the judge under AQHA rules.

In either type of show, the pleasure horse should have a good strong, flat-footed walk; his jog should be smooth, easy and slow the lope should be slow and easy. When asked, the horse should b able to trot on out quietly and to gallop on out without showing anxiety or nervousness. The horse should stop quietly upon com mand from any gait, stand quietly at halt or when the rider mount or dismounts, and should back easily. He should always be on th correct lead at the lope and increase or decrease his gait and pac without over-use of bit or spur on the rider's part.

This horse must be a pleasure to ride. It is important to remem ber that most people who ride this type of horse, or show him, ar not finished horsemen, thus rendering it even more important tha the horse have excellent manners, whether he is showing by himsel or with other horses.

Ring procedure: Horses enter at a walk; and may be aske to walk, jog, trot out, lope, gallop out, halt, each way of the ring The transitions of gaits may be in any order. The reverse is gen erally not asked for until the walk, jog and lope have been done Then the same procedure is requested in the reverse direction. I the judge wishes, the class may be required to halt and back, indivi dually or collectively. Rider may be asked to dismount and mount The mount and dismount and the back are often requested from the line-up in the center of the ring.

Showing: In this particular event, remember you are showing a horse equally at home ridden either by itself or with other horses so any display of ill manners, such as kicking, biting, is especiall undesirable here. Your horse should be entirely independent of wha another horse does and should not be upset, for example, if anothe horse races by. Your horse should have a good, frank walk; neve break gait; the jog should be easy and slow; the lope slow and well balanced. Your horse may work either on contact or with a loose rein, depending upon the customs in the part of the country i which the show is held. If the judge asks for a loose rein at any gait, your horse should remain in balance and neither forge ahead nor drop back. Your horse's head should be quiet. Continual slinging or tossing of the head and fussing at the bit proably may be scored down by the judge. It is no pleasure to a rider to have to constantly fight a horse, and this is a *pleasure* class.

Judging: As in any class, the judging here should be done with complete objectivity, with the judges scoring as if they had neve seen any of the animals before they entered the gate for the class. judging only on what takes place now, with no preconceived ideas.

Two questions mentally asked by the judge of himself can help in the decision of placing this class:

1) Would I enjoy riding this animal?

2) Could I, without anxiety, let my friend, my wife, or child ride this horse?

On the whole, the pleasure horse must be suitable for the novice rider.

It is not difficult for the judge to pick a good ground-covering walk, to not the degree of ease and grace with which a horse performs. Obedience is important, as are manners and the ability of the horse to provide a pleasant, non-irritating ride, easy gaited and attentive to rider's wishes. Too often, however, a judge, passing over a good, pleasant horse, will give the 30% conformation more emphasis than it is entitled to. But if you are showing and this happens to your horse, remember, such an evaluation is your judge's perrogative.

AQHA

WESTERN RIDING HORSE CONTEST
(This class receives half points.)

No horse shall be allowed to show in more than one registered riding horse contest per show.

No show may have both an approved Western Riding class and an approved Trail Horse class.

This contest is neither a stunt nor a race. It is a competition in the performance and characteristics of a good, sensible, well-mannered, free and easy moving ranch horse which can get a man around on the usual ranch chores, over the trails, or give a quiet, comfortable and pleasant ride in open country through and over obstacles. Any western equipment of the exhibitor's choice may be used; but the kind of equipment apparently necessary for the control of the animal, such as severe bit, spurs, tie-down and the like, may be considered by the judge in making awards. Extra credit will not be given for expensive, fancy or parade equipment of the animal or dress of the rider.

All animals entered in a class to be judged must be assembled at the entrance to the arena in ample time for the judging to start promptly and to continue without delay, and shall remain here (except while competing until dismissed by the judge, unless the judge shall otherwise direct. A tardy contestant may be denied competition.

The contesting animals will be judged on riding qualities of gaits (walk, trot, and lope) and movement; response to the rider; manners; disposition; intelligence. Conformation will not be judged.

No more than two classes divided by age are permitted at any one contest.

The Association from time to time will prescribe a pattern and routine according to which the animals shall be worked, and, until changed, the following pateern and routine are prescribed. In order to make fair competition of animals possible it is essential that exhibitors and judge adhere hereto.

On the pattern the short, single line marked "G" represents a swinging gate which the animal on entering the arena, must put the rider in a position to open, pass through and close without dismounting. The gate may be located in any convenient part of the arena where it will not interfere with the balance of the routine. The ten small circles (o) represent markers (barrels, kegs, or standards recommended). These should be separated by uniform distance of not less than thirty nor more than fifty feet. The two short crossed double lines represent obstacles (small logs recommended) just high enought to break the animal's stride in going over. The long and sometimes twisting line indicates the direction to travel and the gaits at which the animals must move. The dotted line (. . . .) indicates the walk, the dashed line (- - - -) the trot, and the solid line (————————) the lope. On entering the arena the exhibitor will put his animal through the gate and then proceed on the routine as indicated by the pattern. On completion he will ride to the judge and back his animal as indicated by the judge. The judge may require an evhibitor to repeat or reverse any part of the routine.

The Western Riding Event of AQHA is similar to the Western Trail Horse event of AHSA. Both are judged on the manners of the horse; quality of his gaits and movements; his response to rider his disposition and intelligence; ability to change leads and direc tions smoothly and quietly and to manipulate the gate and the ride is opening without losing it, and to go over obstacles. Appointment of the rider and conformation of the horse are not scored unde AQHA rules. Essentially here, the judge is looking for a good work ing horse — the type most commonly found on the ranch.

Ring procedure is given above.

Showing: In this class, remember that you should always have one hand on the gate when maneuvering it and that losing you hand's contact with the gate is a fault. Your horse should be quie and should place you wherever you need to be placed to work the gate. (Unfortunately, all gates are not set up correctly, some being too high, too low, or swung with a tilt).

Gaits of the horse in this event should be steady and frank. The log is placed to necessitate a break in gait and to see how the horse will go over it. The jog, depending greatly on the locale of the show will be either the slow, easy jog of the plains country or the long ground-covering trot of the high country. The direction change re quired by the barrels should be smooth and easy with no break in gait; the leads at the lope should be correct; the lope quiet and smooth. At each change of direction, the horse should be able to make his change of leads — this should be anywhere from one to five feet from the approaching barrel, this leeway allowing for where the horse's stride will fall.

Judging: This class may also be judged from the "would I like to be on this horse riding cross-country" angle. The horse's gait should be true, the animal should be quiet, obedient, well-mannered light on the bit, responsive to the rider. Conformation is not judged The ability of the horse to change his leads at the proper time, showing his shiftiness and ability to keep his feet under him, is important. The halt should be balanced, the horse's back straight, and his mouth should remain closed, light and soft to the bit. This class should be ridden either on a contact rein (taking the slack out) or with a moderately loose rein.

AHSA

WESTERN TRAIL HORSES

Working. In all classes in this section horses are to be shown at a walk, jog trot and lope both ways of the ring, on a reasonably loose rein without undue restraint. Entries shall be penalized for being on the wrong lead. Special emphasis shall be placed on the walk. Trail horses must work over and through obstacles.

Obstacles. Without losing control, rider should open a gate, pass through, and close it. The gate handle should not be less than 48" from the ground. Other tests which may be required are: carrying objects from one part of the arena to another; riding through water, over logs or simulated brush; riding down into and up out of ditch without lunging or jumping or jumping; crossing a bridge; backing through obstacles; mounting and dismounting from either side and performing over any natural conditions encountered along the trail.

Generally this event is worked in two sections on the obstacle course and in the ring (on the rail). Either may be first, according to the show conditions. A typical trail or obstacle course is shown above.

Performance is to scored 60% with emphasis on the horse's manners (the quietness, smoothness, obedience with which he performs at each obstacle), 20% is on appointments, neatness and equipment of horse and rider, with 20% going to conformation of the horse. This class, like the AHSA pleasure horse class, is not limited to any breed or combination of breds, and the conformation percentage should be scored with the horse's own breed or type in mind, the type favored being the Western horse.

Ring procedure: The riders may enter the ring, first walk, jog, lope both ways of the ring, mount and dismount from either side, or they may be called upon to work the obstacle course first.

Showing: In showing in this event, the rider's clothes should be neat and clean; the horse, as in all classes, should be in show shape, the equipment, dress and appointments should be neat (gaudiness, silver or any accoutrements other than what would be considered working dress are not essential). The horse should be obedient and ready for anything the Show Committee thinks up for the course; he should be well mannered, alert, responsive. He should be counted on to act intelligently under whatever circumstances arise — and they may be quite unusual! The horse should be able to hold his gaits and his pace and be consistently well balanced in them.

Judging: In this class it is possible for a judge to give a point value to each obstacle that is gone over, under or through. The whole sum of this point score, however, should not exceed 60% of of the whole score and may even be 50%, allowing 10% to come of the rail work. The judge should keep his eyes open for a horse that is obedient yet alert enough to sense danger and one that is responsive to the rider's demands. Neatness of the rider and equipment for the horse count here. As a rule, a rope is carried; a slicker may be. If split reins are used, no hobbles are required. Different parts of the country have different requirements, peculiar to their area, and of course the visiting judge should know them. For instance, the Southwest seldom calls for a slicker, whereas in Northern shows it is mandatory.

A judge may be inclined to place a horse high that is too much in the bit. If you are a judge, remember, a trail horse should be able to drop his head down and size up a situation; although, too often, a horse that wants to move on, if allowed a "too-loose" rein, will take off for parts unknown.

Two other events are listed in the Western Division of AHSA, Western Pleasure Horse Pair Class and Western Equitation. The former is an event in which two horses are judged as a matched pair, with percentages on comformation, tack, equipment and performance.

Ill. 51

Clutch, owned and shown by Mrs. P. J. Gough Jr., high-score Western Trail AHSA.

TRAIL HORSE CLASS
(This class receives half points)

No horse shall be allowed to show in more than one registered Trial Horse class per show.

No show may have both an approved Trail Horse class and an approved Western Riding class.

Horses are to be shown at a walk, jog trot, and lope, both ways of the ring on a reasonably loose rein, without undue restraint. Also, horses are to be shown over and through obstacles.

    a. Without losing control, rider should open a gate, pass through, and close it. The gate handle should not be less than 48 inches from the ground.

    b. Other tests which may be required are: carrying objects from one part of the arena to another; riding through water, over logs, or simulated brush; riding down into and up out of ditch without lunging or jumping; crossing a bridge; backing through obstacles; mounting and dismounting from either side, and performing over any natural conditions eicountered along the trail.

The Trail Horse class is to be judged on performance, with emphasis on manners 60%, appointments, equipment, neatness (silver not to count) 20%; and conformation 20%. Entries may be judged for soundness and conformation before entering the arena.

Entries shall be shown with a stock saddle, but silver equipment will not count over a good working outfit. A rain slicker may be required provided it is so stipulated in the prize list.

There shall be no discrimination against any type of Western bit, but no hackamore, hackamore bit, or other device except a standard Western bit shall be allowed. A curb, half-breed, or spade bit is permissible, but a bosal or cavesson-type noseband, martingale, or tie-down is prohibited. No wire, chain or other metal or rawhide device may be used in conjuction with, or as part of, the leather chin strap.

If split reins are used and horse is broken to ground tying, no hobbles are necessary, but if closed reins are used and a horse is hobble broken, hobble must be carried.

STOCK SEAT EQUITATION SECTION
Seat and Hands

(a) General. Riders will be judged on seat, hands, performance of horse, appointments of horse and rider and suitability of horse to rider.

Results as shown by the performance of the horse are NOT to be considered more important than the method used in obtaining them. There are certain recognized patterns of showing a stock horse in a ring and these patterns should be adhered to. I nother words, a stock horse seat equitation class is a modified version of an open stock horse class and largely governed by rules of the latter. Good hands are paramount.

(b) Mounting and Dismounting. To mount stand facing rear of the horse with reins in left hand placed on horse's neck in front of the withers and with romal or end of the reins on the near side. Grasp stirrup with right hand, place left foot in stirrup, then grasp saddle horn with right hand and mount.

If a romal is used it should be moved to the side of horse after mounting. End of split reins should remain on near side at all times.

If rider uses right hand on rein, the rope should be carried on the near side of the horse; the romal should remain on the near side at all times; and the end of split reins should be moved to off side.

To dismount reverse above procedure and step down facing the horse's head.

(c) Hands. In repose, arms are in a straight line with body, the one holding reins bent at elbow. Only one hand is to be used for reining and hands shall not be changed. Hand to be around reins. Fingers between reins not permitted when using a romal. When using split reins one finger between reins will be permitted. Reins to be above pommel and as near to it as possible. The hand not being used for reining should rest on the outside of rider's thigh (see figure 2) and rider may hold the romal to keep it from swinging and to adjust the position of the rein provided it is held at least 14" from the reining hand (see figure 1). Bracing against horn or coiled reata will be penalized. **Except in Medal Classes, show management may, according to local condition, designate whether a romal or split reins are to be used, provided it is so stipulated in the prize list.**

(d) Basic Position. The rider should sit the saddle with legs hanging straight and slightly forward to stirrups, or with knees slightly bent and weight directly over balls of feet. In either position the stirrup should be just short enough to allow heels to be lower than toes. Body always should appear comfortable, relaxed and flexible. Feet should be placed in the stirrups with weight on ball of the foot. Consideration, however, should be given to the width of the stirrups, which vary on Western saddles. If stirrups are wide, the foot may have the appearance of being "home" when in reality the weight is being properly carried on the ball of the foot.

(e) Position in Motion. Rider should sit to jog and not post. At the lope he should be close to the saddle. All movements of horse should be governed by the use of imperceptible aids, and the shifting of rider's weight is not desirable.

Appointments

(a) Personal. Clothing must be clean, workmanlike and neat. Riders to wear western hat and cowboy boots. Management may designate whether chaps are to be used, according to local conditions. Tapaderos and spurs are optional.

(b) Tack. The saddle must fit the rider. It may be slick or swelled fork, have a high or low cantle, but must definitely be sized to the rider. A half-breed, spade or curb bit may be used, but no wire, chain or other metal or rawhide device is permissible in conjuction with or as part of the leather chin strap. Hackamores, tie-downs, running martingales and draw reins are prohibited. If closed reins are used, hobbles must be carried; if split reins are used and horse is broken to ground tie, no hobbles are necessary. Bosals or Cavesson-type nosebands are prohibited. A rope or reata must be carried. Silver equipment may be used but shall not be given preference over good working equipment. The use of shoes other than standard horse shoes is to be discouraged and may be penalized by the judge.

Class Routine. Horses are to enter ring at a walk and be judged at a walk, jog and lope. They shall be worked both ways of the ring and shall always be on the correct lead. Individual performances shall follow the pattern as outlined in the Western Division, Rule XXXIII, Part II, Sec. 2. The horse should be in perfect balance at all times, working entirely off his haunches. Neck and head should be in a direct line with body, mouth closed and head at normal height. If the horse works off hind quarters at all times and in a straight line, all possibility of draw-reining will be avoided. It must be remembered that, above all a stock horse is one that responds instantly and smoothly to all aids. Rider shall be asked to dismount and mount. It is inadvisable to change horses due to difficulty of properly fitting the tack.

Requirements for Specific Classes. Riders should be able to perform not only the ring routine demanded of them but also should be able to perform whatever additional tests the judge may deem advisable to ask of them. Horses shall be required to back in a straight line in all classes. Other individual performance is optional in all Stock Seat Equitation Classes except AHSA Medal and Championship Classes in which the entire routine is required.

All classes except Medal Classes may be divided as to age and as to boys and girls. In the event management wishes to divide classes as to age the following divisions are recommended but may be varied according to local conditions.

Figure 1

137

(a) For Junior Riders who have not reached their 14th birthday.

(b) For Junior Riders who have reached their 11th but not their 14th birthday.

(c) For Junior Riders who have reached their 14th but not their 18th Birthday.

1. AHSA Medal Class. For Junior Riders who have not reached their 18th birthday. (See Rule XXXIV)

2. Maiden, Novice and Limit. For Junior Riders who have not reached their 18th birthday. (See Rule XII, Part III, Sec. 2 (e).

3. Open. For Junior Riders who have not reached their 18th birthday.

4. Championship—To be awarded on a competitive basis. May be held (a) as a (free) post entry class, open to any designated number of place winners (minimum of two) in previous classes in this section of the Division except Maiden, Novice and Limit classes, or (b) as an open class with advance entries. To be eligible, riders must have competed in at least one other class in this section of the Division (In either case winners of first and second places shall receive Champion and Reserve Champion ribbons.)

Individual performance is required of all contestants.

This Western equitation class should be studied carefully by the judges, for here is where the reinsmen, the horsemen, of the

Figure 2

future start. A judge should bear in mind that the horse's perform-ance should not be scored higher than the skill of the junior rider. The rider's hands are of prime importance in this class. Horseman-ship is the chief factor, even if the horse performs as precisely as a push-button machine.

Rules, class procedure, showing and judging are clearly set forth in Sec. 1 through 3.

For Younger Riders:

Thought the AQHA has no junior horsemanship events, many shows have Western Equitation with the age breaks as follows: 6 and under, lead line; 8 and under, walk, trot; walk, trot, lope for 9 and under, 11 and under, 12-14 and 15-17, or any age break from 1 to 17. The customary two-age break lists 12 and under and 13-17.

A typical list of such events is that of the show held at Roswell, N.M. in June of each year:

Reining: 11 and under
                12-14
                15-17
Barrels: 11 and under
                12-14
                15-17
Lead line: 6 and under
Western Trail: 17 and under
Equitation Stock Seat: 11 and under
                              12-14
                              15-17
Stock Horse: 11 and under
              12-14
              15-17
Western Pleasure: 17 and under
Consolation Horsemanship (non-winners in a horsemanship class of this show)

It seem appropriate at this time to list the main points at Show-manship at Halter under the Youth Activities of the AQHA. This class has done a great deal toward developing not only the child's ability to fit a horse but to show it properly and thus properly evalu-ate the horse.

AQHA

SHOWMANSHIP AT HALTER

Listed below are points on which youth shows are to be judged. Only showman to be judged. The horse is merely a prop to show the ability of the showman.

APPEARANCE OF HORSE .... 40 Points
a. Condition and Thriftiness (15 Points)
b. Grooming (15 Points)
    1. Hair coat clean, well brushed.
    2. Mane and tail free of tangles and clean.
    3. Hoofs trimmed properly. If shod, shoes must fit properly

and clinches should be neat.

c. Trimming (5 Points)
   1. Quarter Horse manes may be roached, but foretop and tuft over withers must be left.
   2. Quarter Horse tails should be thinned and shortened to hock length.
   3. Inside of ears may be clipped.
   Long hair on jaw, and legs and pasterns should be clipped.
d. Tack (5 Points)
   Tack should be neat, clean and in good repair.

APPEARANCE OF EXHIBITOR .... 10 Points
Clothes and person — neat and clean.
Suitable western riding clothes.

SHOWING HORSE IN RING .... 50 Points
a. Leading (15 Points)
   1. Enter ring leading animal at an alert walk in a counter-clockwise direction. Walk on animal's left side, holding lead shank in right hand, near halter. The remaining portion of lead is held neatly coiled in left hand. Animal should lead readily at a walk or trot.
   2. After judge has lined up the class in front of spectators, he will call on each exhibitor to move his horse individually. When moving the horse, allow him sufficient lead so that he can move freely and in a straight line. Lead the horse from the left side the required distance, turn to the right around the horse and lead directly back to the judge. Be sure that the judge gets a clear unobstructed view of the horses' action. Set your horse up squarely in front of the judge for his inspection and after being released, move promptly to your position in line.
b. Posing (15 Points)
   1. When posing your horse, stand toward the front facing the horse, but always in a position where you can keep your eye on the judge.
   2. Pose Quarter Horses with their feet squarely under them. Do most of the showing with lead strap. Never kick horse's leg into position.
   3. Do not crowd the exhibitor next to you when in a side by side position. Do not crowd exhibitor in front when lined up head to tail.
   4. When judge is observing other animals, let yours stand if reasonably well.
   5. Be natural, overshowing, undue fussing and maneuvering are objectionable.
c. Poise, Alertness, and Merits (20 Points)
   1. Keep alert and be aware of the position of the judge at all times. Don't be distracted by persons or things outside the ring.
   2. Show animal at all times, not yourself.
   3. Respond quickly to requests from judge and officials.
   4. Be courteous and sportsmanlike at all times.
   5. Recignize quickly and correct faults of horses.
   6. Keep showing until the entire class has been placed and has been excused from the ring.

   No stallions will be used in the Showmanship at Halter class.

140

Chapter XI

SHOWS AND SHOWING
(Reining, Working, Roping, Cutting, etc.)

If pleasure classes in general are suitable for the novice rider on the schooled horse, the events treated in this chapter call for highly developed skill on the part of both rider and horse, even, in events like roping where only the horse's performance is scored.

Roping, AQHA: There is no comparable class in AHSA. The importance of this class, and its reason for being in the AQHA list is events, is based on the fact that the quarter horse is essentially a working horse, that is, a horse that works for his living, whether on the range roping a wormy calf, in the branding pens dragging a yearling to the fire, or in the rodeo arena.

CALF ROPING CONTEST

No horse shall be allowed to show in more than one approved AQHA registered calf roping class per show.

A calf roping contest will be held under the usual common rodeo standards and conditions. Horse must start from behind a barrier.

Scoring will be done on the basis of 60-80 with 70 denoting an average performance.

Only the performance of the horse is to count. Time of the roper will not count for or against the horse. A time limit of two minutes for each contestant will be allowed.

The roper may throw as many loops in this two minutes as necessary to effectively show his horse. If more than one loop is thrown, however, the roper must carry second rope tied to saddle which is to be used for the second loop. Should roper desire to throw the third, or more loops, he may recoil either rope.

If roper carries only one rope and misses on first loop, he must retire from arena with no score (this provision is necessary to show that horse will work trailing a rope).

The horse will be judged on manners behind the barrier, scoring speed to calf, rating calf, the stop, working the rope and his manners while roper is returning to horse after tie has been made.

Breaking the barrier, or any unnecessary whipping, jerking reins, talking or any noise making, slapping, jerking rope, or any unnecessary action to induce the horse to perform better, will be considered a fault and scored accordingly.

STEER ROPING CONTEST

A horse shall be allowed to show in Heading or Heeling, or both. It must be declared before the horse enters the arena, however, in which event the horse is competing during that run.

A steer roping contest will be held under the usual common rodeo standards and conditions.

Three different kinds of steer roping are acceptable as approved events. These are Team Tying, Dally Team Roping, and Dally Steer Stopping. No show may have more than one type of steer roping approved.

Team Tying
(Rope tied "hard and fast")

The heading horse and the heeling horse are to be entered

and scored individually, not as a team.

A contestant may ride only one horse in a class. A horse shall be allowed to show in Heading or Heeling, or both, but must specify which one before the run. When two or more go-rounds are held, each team of horses and ropers must be the same and work in identical and consecutive order.

Team tying horses shall be scored on the basis of 60 to 80 points with 70 denoting an average performance.

The heading horses shall be started behind a barrier; also the heeling horses if the judge so wishes. The header must head the steer and the heeler must heel the steer. Horses can not switch positions. There is a time limit of two minutes or two loops, which ever comes first. (Each roper of a team is entitled to two loops or two minutes.) If a second loop is thrown, the roper must carry a second rope tied to the saddle which is to be used for the second loop.

Horse or horses will be judged on manners behind the barrier and at all other times. The heading horse shall be judged on the rate of speed to steer, ability of horse to rate, check, turn, and set steer in position for heeler. The heeling horse will be judged on ease of manner in which he turns and prepares for heel's position to throw loop, jerk steer, and make him accessible for header to tie.

Breaking the barrier, or any unnecessary whipping, jerking reins, talking or any noise making, slapping, jerking rope, or any unnecessary action to induce the horse to perform better, will be considered a fault and scored accordingly.

Legal catches are both horns, half head, and around neck. Any front leg in the catch is not legal. Heel catch must be on one or both hind legs. Any double knot tied above heels and below hocks is a legal tie. Steer must be down to make a legal tie, and header must tie the steer.

Dally Team Roping

The heading horse and the heeling horse are to be entered and scored individully, not as a team.

The heading horses shall be started behind a barrier; also heeling horses if the judge so wishes.

Dally Team Roping horses shall be scored on the basis of 60 to 80 points with 70 denoting an average performance.

There is a time limit of two minutes or two loops, whichever comes first. (Each roper of a team is entitled to two loops or two minutes.) Roper may not carry a second rope; should be desire to use a second loop, he may recoil rope. The header must head the steer and the heeler must heel the steer.

Horse or horses will be judged on manners behind the barrier, and at all other times. The heading horse shall be judged on the rate of speed to steer, ability of horse to rate, check, turn, and set steer in position for heeler. The heeling horse will be judged on ease of manner in which he turns and prepares for heeler's position to throw loop, jerk steer and keep rope tight in a backing position.

Breaking the barrier, or any unnecessary whipping, jerking reins, talking or any noise making, slapping, jerking rope, or any unnecessary action to induce the horse to perform better, will be considered a fault and scored accordingly.

Legal catches are both horns, half head, and around neck.

Any front leg in the catch is not legal. Heel catch may be one or both hind legs.

Dally Steer Stopping

A contestant may ride only one horse in a class.

The horse shall be started behind barrier and scored on a basis of 60 to 80 points with 70 denoting an average performance.

There is a time limit of two minutes or two loops, whichever comes first.

Horse will be judged on manners behind the barrier and at all other times. The horse shall be judged on the rate of speed to steer, ability of horse to rate, check, stop straight, and to stop and turn the steer to face horse.

Breaking the barrier, or any unnecessary whipping, jerking reins, talking or any noise making, slapping, jerking rope, or any unnecessary ction to induce the horse to perform better, will be considered a fault and scored accordingly.

Legal catches are both horns, half head, and round neck. Any front leg in the catch is not legal.

Ring procedure: Each contestant is called individually, working under standard rodeo procedure. Instead of time being important, paramount are the manners of the horse behind the barrier and while working, his ability to follow the calf, rate behind it, and to stop and work the rope. These play a greater part in the score than the ability of the rider to throw a good loop.

Judging: The judging score of this class is between 60-80, with 70 being an average performance. It takes a good judge to appreciate a horse that is working correctly and with skill, regardless of how good or bad his rider. Too often, a horse is scored down because of rider error. A man who has been a contestant in roping is best able to judge this class fairly. Such a judge knows a horse should be ready but able to stand the test of behaving before the barrier is snapped (10 seconds is costly for a broken barrier at a rodeo); the horse must get to that calf, check and rate himself to give the roper a fair chance to drop him rope, and must stop and hold the calf when caught, face him and keep the rope taut regardless of the ruckus the crowd is making. The horse must be able to handle any unexpected situation that comes up, such as getting a rope around his forefoot, his rider falling, etc. It takes a roper to appreciate a good roping horse.

Reining Class, AQHA: (This class is similar to the AHSA Stock Horse, Sec. A — When Not Worked on Cattle, rules for which will be given later.)

REINING CONTEST

No horse shall be allowed to show in more than one approved AQHA registered reining class per show.

All contestants concerned will gather at the arena at the proper time. Upon call, each contestant will perform the required pattern individually and separately.

Each horse will be judged on the neatness, dispatch, ease, calmness and speed with which it performs the pattern.

Excessive jawing, open mouth or head raising on stop, lack of smooth sliding stop on haunches, breaking gaits, refusing to change lead, anticipating signals, stumbling or falling, wringing tail, backing sideways, knocking over stakes or kegs, changing hands on reins, losing stirrups, or holding on, or two hands on reins, or any unnecessary aid given by the rider to the horse (such as unnecessary talking, petting, spurring, quirting, jerking of reins, etc.), to induce the horse to perform will be considered a fault and scored accordingly.

Horse shall rein and handle easily, fluently, effortlessly, and with reasonable speed throughout the pattern.

Any horse not following exact pattern will be disqualified.

Scoring will be on the basis of 60-80 with 70 denoting an average performance.

In case of doubt, a judge may require any contestant to repeat his performance of any or all the various parts of the pattern.

A judge shall have the authority to require the removal or alteration of any piece of equipment or accoutrement which, in his opinion, would tend to give a horse an unfair advantage. Any inhumane equipment will be scored accordingly.

A show may have up to three approved reining classes. If three reining classes are to be held at a show, they shall be the following:

    (a) Senior Reining (five years olds and older, all horses must be shown with bit.)

    (b) Junior Bit Reining (four year olds and younger, all horses to be shown with bit.)

    (c) Hackamore Reining (four year olds and younger, all horses to be shown with hackamore.)

If two reining classes are to be held at a show, they shall be the following:

    (a) Senior Reining (five year olds and older, all horses must be shown with bit).

    (b) Junior Reining (four year olds and younger, horses may be shown with either bit or hackamore at the discretion of the exhibitor). Riders may use only one hand on reins.

If only one reining class is to be held at a show, it shall be the following:

    (a) Reining (all ages — horses five years old and older must be shown in bit; horses four years old and younger may be shown in either bit or hackamore at the discretion of the exhibitor).

In straight hackamore classes, two hands may be used. In combined bit and hackamore classes, only one hand on reins of bit or hackamore.

For HACKAMORE REINING, horses will be ridden ONLY with a rawhide braided or leather braided or rope bosal. Absolutely no iron will be permitted under the jaws regardless of how padded or taped.

For BIT REINING, horses will be ridden with grazing, snaffle curb, half-breed, bar or spade bit. However, no wire curbs, regardless of how padded or taped, or no chin strap narrower than one- half inch, or no nose bands or tiedowns will be permitted.

Chain curbs are permissible but must be at least one-half inch in width, can not be twisted, and must meet the approval of the judge.

Horses, five years old and older, must perform in the bit reining class.

Faults Against the Horse.

1. Opening mouth excessively in Bit Reining.
2. Breaking gaits.
3. Refusing to change leads.
4. Anticipating signals.

5. Stumbling and falling.
6. Wringing tail.
7. Bouncing or sideways stop.
8. Backing sideways.

Faults Against the Rider
1. Changing hands on reins.
2. Losing stirrup.
3. Two hands on reins at any time.
4. Any unnecessary aid given by the rider to the horse (such as unnecessary talking, petting, spurring, quirting, jerking of reins, etc.), to induce the horse to perform will be considered a fault and scored accordingly.

In an approved Reining class, any one of the three approved AQHA Reining Patterns may be used: Number 1, Number 2, or Number 3. One of these three patterns is to be selected by the judge of the class and used by all contestants in the class.

The arena or plot should be approximately 50 x 150 feet in size and the judge will indicate where to place the markers.

Ride pattern as follows:
1. to 2. Run at full speed (should be run at least 20 feet from any fence or wall).
2. Stop and back.
3. Settle horse for 10 seconds.
4. & 5. Ride small figure 8 at slow canter.
6. & 7. Ride large figure 8 fast.
8. Left roll back over hocks. Upright markers are mandatory at points marked X on the pattern.
9. Right roll back over hocks.
10. Stop

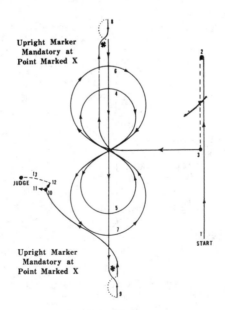

Pattern 1

145

11. Pivot left.
12. Pivot right.
13. Walk to judge and stop for inspection until dismissed.

The arena or plot should be approximately 50x150 feet in size. The judge shall indicate with markers on arena fence or wall the length of the pattern, but kegs or other markers within the area of the pattern will not be used.

Ride pattern as follows:

1. to 2. Run at full speed (should be run at least 20 feet from any fence or wall).
2. Stop and back.
3. Settle horse for 10 seconds.
4. & 5. Ride two circles to the right.
6. & 7. Ride two circles to the left.
8. Proceed to the area beyond the point indicated by the marker on the arena wall or fence and do a left roll back over the hocks.
9. Proceed to the area beyond the point indicated by the other marker on the arena wall or fence and do a right roll back over the hocks.
10. Stop.
11. Pivot left.
12. Pivot right.
13. Walk to judge and stop for inspection untill dismissed.

The arena or plot should be approximately 50 x 150 feet in size. The judge shall indivate with markers on arena fence or wall the

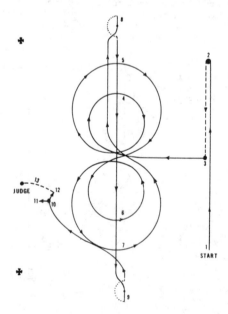

✚ Mandatory marker on arena fence or wall.

Pattern 2

146

length of the pattern, but kegs or other markers within the area of the pattern will not be used.
Ride pattern as follows:

1. to 2. Run at full speed (should be run at least 20 feet from any fence or wall).
2. Stop.
3. Do a 360 degree spin.
4. Hesitate.
5. Proceed to the area beyond the point indicated by the marker on the arena wall or fence and do a left roll back over the hocks.
6. Stop.
7. Do a 360 degree spin.
8. Hesitate.
9. Proceed to the area beyond the point indicated by the other marker on the arena wall or fence and do a right roll back over the hocks.
10. & 11. Ride a figure 8.
12. to 13. Run at full speed.
13. Sliding stop.
13. to 14. Back.
15. Walk to judge and stop for inspection until dismissed.

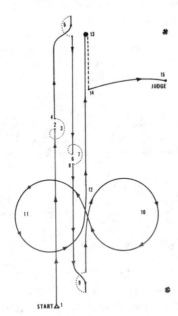

✤ Mandatory marker on arena fence or wall.

Pattern 3

147

Showing: In most events, the rider only helps or hinders the paramount performer, the horse, and the reining class is no exception. Here the rider should show in accordance with the horse's ability. If the horse is a young one and can only work well in slow agits, then the rider should show him that way. Trying to force will more than likely make the horse blow up, with a loss to his trainer of several months of schooling, not to mention a loss in score. Remember: *work your horse at the speed at which he can do each and every movement correctly.*

The rider should give the appearance of oneness with the horse, and the horse should give the appearance of being able to do any movement the rider may ask. The horse should not be "pattern happy" but he should be "rider conscious". At the stop, the horse should be well balanced, with correct head position, feet well under him, mouth closed, back straight and not labored. The figure eights should be well defined, regular circles, with a change of leads in the middle. The horse should not duck or cheat his turns. Coming out of the circle on the left lead, the horse should change to the right lead and, at the marker, check and roll back over his hicks to the left. In rolling back over his hocks, he should give the appearance of sitting down on his hind legs, which are planted in one spot, with the forehand swinging up and around the stationary hindquarters. Coming off in a left lead, the horse may or may not hold this lead, depending on his balance and direction change from the first rollback. Galloping into the other end on a left lead, he should hold this lead and not switch leads until he goes around the second marker. Here again he checks, pivots around hindquarters, and comes out on the opposite lead or right lead. If there is a change of direction to the judge, the horse should change leads. If there is no change of direction, the rider will take him up to the judge, halt again, smoothly balanced, the horse's mouth closed and his body in a straight line. After the stop, the horse should offset or pivot left and then right, easily and uickly, with his feet under him, pivoting his forehand about the hindquarters. Then, jogging up to the judge, he should stand quietly, allowing the judge to inspect the equipment.

Judging: Essentially, the judge is looking for a well-mannered, light-mouthed, responsive horse that can handle at a reasonable speed and still be obedient. The ability of the horse on his feet, his ability to change leads, the correctness of each movement, and his manner, each are important. Rough hands on the part of the rider, unnecessary perking and spurring, all relate adversely to the ability of the horse to work correctly. If it is necessary to subject a horse to such conditions, he either has no mouth or no schooling.

148

STOCK HORSE SECTION
General

Horses shall be of any breed or combination of breeds 14.1 hands and over, serviceably sound, in good condition and of stock horse type. A full mane is not required. Entries may be judged for soundness and conformation before entering the arena. The use of shoes other than standard horse shoes is to be discouraged and may be penalized by the Judge.

Appointments

(a) Personal. Riders wear Western hat, chaps, shotgunchaps or chinks, cowboy boots and carry a rope or reata. Spurs are optional. A rain slicker may be required in Trail and Pleasure classes provided it is so stipulated in the prize list.

(b) Tack. (1) Stock Horse Classes. Entries shall be shown with stock saddle without tapaderos. Management may designate type of western bit to be used according to local conditions. Bosals or cavesson-type noseband, martingale, choke rope and tie-down are prohibited. No wire, chain or other metal or rawhide device may be used in conjuction with, or as part of, leather chin strap.

(2) Trail and Pleasure Horse Classes. Entries shall be shown with a stock saddle, but silver equipment will not count over a good working outfit. There shall be no discrimination against any type of Western bit. No hackamore, hackamore bit or other device except a standard Western bit without joints shall be allowed. A curb, halfbreed or spade bit is permissible but a bosal or cavesson-type noseband, martingale or tie-down is prohibited. No wire, chain or other metal or rawhide device may be used in conjuction with, or as part of, the leather chin strap. If split reins are used no hobbles are necessary but if closed reins are used hobbles must be carried.

Stock Horse Section

Instruction to Riders. Only one hand may be used for rein-

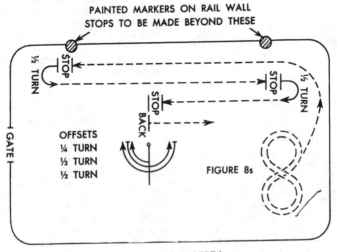

Stock Horse AHSA

Ill. 52

Colonel Bonite Highscore Stock Horse A.H.S.A. owned by Robin L. McCandlish.

ing and hands must not be changed. Hand to be around reins. Fingers between reins not permitted. Spurs or romal shall not be used forward of the cinch. While horse is in motion rider's hands shall be clear of horse and saddle. (Judge should instruct exhibitors to keep hands clear of saddle except when it is necessary to use them to prevent a fall.) Riders may be disqualified for not following a judge's instructions. Two or more horses may be entered by the same exhibitor, who may elect to show each of them personally in individual workouts.

Working.

(a) When not worked on cattle. The suggested procedure is for horses to enter ring at a walk, taking a jog-trot and slow lope upon request. They then shall line up or retire from the ring at the judge's direction. Horses then shall be worked individually. Rider shall start his workout with a figure eight, executed at a lope two or three times and of sufficient size to avoid short, choppy turns. Failure of horse to change both front and hind leads shall be baulted. The smoother and more even the gait, the more credit to the horse. Entry shall then go to the end of arena, turn and run full length of arena to a straight sliding stop, turn away from the rail and run to the other end of the arena and make a straight sliding stop, turn away from therail, and run to the center of the arena and make a straight, sliding stop. After allowing the horse to

150

gather itself, back the horse in exactly the opposite direction in a straight line for 10-15 fet. Horse shall then be brought up to the judge, stopped and, with weight on the hind quarters and with legs in one position, make a quarter turn to the right, half turn to the left and half turn to the right. After all entries have thus been shown, indicated horses may be worked on a rope sack. (Optional) Sack is to be roped, horse run from side to side, turning squarely back as end of rope is reached with no to exceed 25 feet of rope out, purpose being to show that a horse can work accurately and fast after an animal has been roped, and is not rope shy. If rope or sack is to be used, prize list must so state.

Horses shall be judged on a basis of 100 pts. for a perfect score as follows: Rein work, 50 pts.; conformation, 20 pts.; manners, 20 pts. and appointments, 10 pts.

The foregoing is set up as a guide, but the judge may deviate from this procedure. In classes such as Ladies, Amateur and Green a less severe pattern may be used and horses will still qualify for the chapionship. When complimentary classes (i.e., Lightweight and Heavyweight) are offered the same reining test must be used in each.

In large classes, eliminations or "reining tests" should be held outside the show-ring, and all entries may not be required to undergo all tests if obviously out of consideration for ribbons.

(b) When worked on cattle. Horses shall be worked on reining test as prescribed in (a). In addition, a bunch of cattle shall be held by riders at a convenient place in the arena, track or other area devoted to the purpose. Exhibitor shall work his horse as directed by the judge. Precision, ease and speed with which judge's instructions are carried out shall be considered in rating entries.

Horses shall be judged on a basis of 150 pts. for a perfect score as follows: Cow work, 50 pts.; rein work, 50 pts.; conformation, 20 pts.; manners, 20 pts. and appointments, 10 pts.

Faults. The following characteristics are considered as faults: switching tail, exaggerated opening of mouth, hard or heavy mouth, nervous throwing of head, lugging on bridle, halting or hesitation while being shown, particularly when being run out, indicating anticipation of being set up, which is characteristic of an over-trained horse.

The characteristics of a good working horse are:
1. Good manners.
2. Horse should be shifty, smooth and have his feet under him at all times. When stopping, hind feet should be well under him.
3. Horse should have a soft mouth and should respond to a light rein especially when turning.
4. Head should be maintained in its natural position.
5. Horse should be able to work at reasonable speed and still be under control of the rider.

Falls. Fall of horse and/or rider while being shown in reining tests or while working on cattle shall not eliminate the entry but may be penalized at the judge's discretion.

Jaquima Horses. A Jaquima horse is not more than 5 years old and must never have been shown in a bridle, other than a snaffle bit. Rider may use both hands. Horses shall enter arena and work in the same manner as prescribed for bridle classes, but with less speed and — not to be worked on sack. Deviation from this role with respect to a hore's age or previoos experience in a bridle shall result in disqualification.

Green Stock Horses. A green stock horse is a horse that has not been shown in a stock horse slass prior to January 1st of the current year.

Class Specifications

Stallions are prohibited in Ladies, and Junior Exhibitors Classes.

STOCK HORSES GREEN, LIGHTWEIGHT (850-1100 lbs.), HEAVYWEIGHT (over 1100 lbs.), OPEN. To be shown at a walk, jog trot and lope without restraint, lope a figure eight, run at speed and stop, turn easily. Rope test optional. To be judged on rein, conformation, manners and appointments.

JUNIOR EXHIBITORS' STOCK HORSES. Open to horses or ponies. To be judged as in open classes. Particular attention shall be paid to hands of riders, since a light hand is paramount to becoming a good horseman. To be judged on manners, rein, conformation and appointments.

LADIES' STOCK HORSES. To be shown at a walk, jog trot and lope without restraint, lope a figure eight, run at speed and stop, turn easily. Rope test optional. To be judged on rein, conformation, manners and appointments.

STOCK HORSE CHAMPIONSHIP. To be eligible, horses must be entered, shown and judged in any other class in this section ,or) class shall be composed of not more than 10 entries which shall be the top scoring horses of the show in the stock horse section. To be shown at a walk, jog trot and lope without restraint, lope a figure eight, run at speed and stop, turn easily. Rope test optional. To be judged on rein, conformation, manners and appointments.

JAQUIMA CLASS. Open to horses not over 5 years old. To be shown with jaquima only. To be judged on rein, conformation, manners and appointments.

In this class the horse should handle or work more or less the same as a reining horse. However, the scoring for dry work is 50% rein, 20% conformation, 20% manners, and 10% appointments.

The rules and the ring procedure are listed under 1,2,3,4,5 6.7; B, 1.

Showing: Showing is essentially the same as under AQHA rules, but shown more up in the bridle than in other parts of the country. "In the one slight difference is that the horses in the Far West are generally bridle" could also be called "collected".

Judging: The judge under these rules has percentages to take into consideration, and it can happen that the top working horse loses enough points on conformation and appointments to affect his standing as the first place horse.

Working Cowhorse Contest, AQHA: This class too, is in a sense like the cow work of the AHSA Stock Horse If Cattle Are Used.

WORKING COWHORSE CONTEST

No show may offer this Working Cowhorse class as an approved class for which points will be awarded unless the show also offers an approved Reining class with the AQHA reining pattern.

No horse shall be allowed to show in more than one registered Working Cowhorse class per show.

The approved pattern will be used and each contestant will cause his horse to travel at the gait indicaed for each part of the pattern.

Horses will enter the ring at a walk, taking a jog-trot and slow lope upon request. They then shall line up or retire from the ring at the judge's direction. Horses then shall be worked individually.

Rider shall start his workout with a figure eight, executed at a lope two times and of sufficient size to avoid short, choppy turns. Failure of horses to change both front and hind leads shall be faulted. The smoother and more even the gait, the more credit to the horse.

The entry shall then go to the end of the arena, turn and run full length of the arena, make a straight sliding stop, turn away from the rail, run to the other end of the arena, make a straight sliding stop, turn away from the rail, run to the center of the arena, and make a straight sliding stop.

After allowing the horse to gather itself, back the horse in exactly the apposite direction in a straight line for 10 to 15 feet.

Horse shall then be brought up to the judge, stopped and, with weight on the hind quarters and with hind legs in one position, make a quarter turn to the right, half turn to the left, and half turn to the right. The entry shall then retire from the arena.

The judge may request additional work at his option.

In the event that cattle are to be worked, it shall be so stated in the premium list and the working procedure will be as follows.

One animal shall be turned into the arena and the contestant shall hold the animal at one end of the arena long enough to indicate to the judge that the horse is watching the cow.

The cow shall then be allowed to run down the side of the arena and the contestant shall turn the animal twice each way against the fence. The cow shall then be taken to the center of the arena and circled once each way.

Scoring will be on the basis of 60 to 80, with 70 denoting an average performance. The same basis of scoring shall apply to both the reined work and cow work.

Fall of horse and/or rider while being shown either in cow work or reined work shall not eliminate the entry.

The following characteristics are considered as faults:

a. Switching tail,
b. Exaggerated opening of mouth,
c. Hard or heavy mouth,
d. Nervious throwing of head,
e. Lugging on bridle,
f. Halting or hesitation while being shown, particularly when being run out, indicating anticipation of being set up, which is characteristic of an overtrained horse.
g. Losing a cow or being unable to finish a pattern because of a bad cow, the contestant should be penalized at the judge's discretion.

The characteristics of a good working horse are:

a. Good manners;
b. Horse should be shifty, smooth and have his feet under him at all times; when stopping, hind feet should be well under him;
c. Horse should have a soft mouth and should respond to a light rein, especially when turning;

153

d. Head should be maintained in its natural position;

e. Horse should be able to work at reasonable speed and still be under control of the rider.

Entries shall be shown with stock saddle, without tapaderos. When a bit is used in this class, horses will be ridden with grazing snaffle, curb, half-breed, bar or spade bit. No wire curbs, however, regardless of how padded or taped, or no chin strap narrower than one-half inch, or no nose bands or tiedowns will be permitted. Chain curbs are permissible but must be of the standard flat variety and must meet the approval of the judge.

Rider shall wear western hat, chaps, shotgun chaps, or chinks, cowboy boots, and carry rope or riata. Spurs are optional.

The use of shoes other than standard horseshoes is to be discouraged and may be penalized by the judge.

Only one hand may be used on reins and hands must not be changed. Hand to be around reins. Fingers between reins not permitted. Spurs or romal shall not be used forward of the cinch. While horse is in motion, rider's hands shall be clear of horse and saddle.

Judge should instruct exhibitors to keep hands clear of saddle except when it is necessary to use them to prevent a fall. Riders may be disqualified for not following judge's instructions. Judges should pay particular attention to the hands of juniors, as a light hand is paramount to becoming a good showman of stock horses.

A hackamore horse in the Working Cowhorse class is a horse not more than four years old, and must never have been shown in any class in a bridle, other than a snaffle bit. Rider may use both hands. Horses shall enter arena and work in the same manner as prescribed for bridle classes. Horses will be ridden only with a rawhide braided or leather braided or rope bosal. Absolutely no iron will be permitted under jaws regardless of how padded or taped.

Ride pattern as follows:

a. begin work,

b. first figure eight,

c. second figure eight,

d. begin run,

e. sliding stop,

f. turn away from rail and begin second run,

g. sliding stop,

h. turn away from rail and make short run,

i. sliding stop,

j. back up,

k. quarter turn to right,

l. half turn to left,

m. half turn to right.

Rules, ring showing, and judging procedure are all included above. In showing and judging, special attention should be given to the fact that, though these horses are showing, they should be judged for their working ability, not showmanship. They are portraying what the working ranch horse is supposed to be able to do every day.

Cutting Horse Event: This event is held under AQHA rules or those of the National Cutting Horse Association, the latter open as far as breed is concerned. AQHA. honors points won at ACHA shows and the rules and judges of this association.

A cutting horse is essentially "a stock horse with a high economic value." He can earn his keep at home and go to a contest and present a splendid, entertaining and colorful picture of range work at its best. His performance, regardless of his color, sex or breed, is the sole guide to this horse's value; that is, his ability to enter a herd of cattle, cut an animal out of the herd (for shipment to market, doctoring, moving to another pasture — or for show work) and prevent that animal from returning to the herd. A cutting horse is particularly judged on his natural ability, as he works with a loose rein and maintains the proper balance to be able to move quickly in any direction.

Rules and show procedure are too lengthly to insert here, but they may be obtained from the National Cutting Horse Association, Box 12155, Fort Worth, Texas.

The closest AHSA comes to this event in the use of cattle is the Stock Horse event; but only in the fact that they both use cattle is the AHSA class similar to the cutting horse event. Both requirements and manner of handling are completely different.

* * * *

Timed events could fall in the realm of beginner, intermediate or advanced rider, depending for what purpose that event is used. Barrel races can be used for beginners at the walk or trot or even the slowest cantering time is the winner . . . children as young as five or six are capable of working old reliable horses at timed events.

No timed events fall within the rules of the AHSA, though they have a bulletin out called *Gym-khana Events*, which is a great help to the novice who never grew up in an area that had timed events.

The AQHA recognizes three timed event classes: the barrel race, the stake and pole bending. The barrel race has long been a favorite in the rodeo arena and is a very colorful and thrilling event.

BARREL RACING CONTEST

No horse shall be allowed to show in more than one registered barrel race per show.

Knocking over barrels or failure to follow the course shall cause disqualification. If a rider touches a barrel with his hand, the horse will be disqualified.

The course must be measured exactly. If the course is too large for the available space, then the pattern should be reduced 5 yards at a time until the pattern fits the arena.

REMEMBER TO LEAVE adequate space between barrels and any obstacles. The distance from barrel number 3 to the finish line need not be reduced 5 yards at a time if there is sufficient room for the horses to stop.

Western type equipment must be used. Use of hackamore or other types of bridles is the optional choice of the contestant; however, the timer or judge may prohibit the use of bits or equipment that he may consider severe.

A clearly visible starting line shall be provided, either through the use of a rope buried in the ground or one marked by lime. At least two watches shall be used with the average time of the watches used by the official timers to be the official time. The barrel race contest is strictly a timed event.

In the event of a tie, the horse declared the winner in the

runoff must run the pattern within two seconds of its original time or the runoff must be held again.

Remember to set your course so that a horse may have ample room to turn and stop.

Instructions for AQHA Barrel Course

The contestant is allowed a running start. Timing shall begin as soon as the horse's nose reaches the starting line and will be stopped when the horse's nose passes over the finish line.

At a signal from the starter or times, such as the word "go," the contestant will go to barrel number 1 passing to the left of this barrel, complete a 360 degree turn, then on to barrel number 2, this time passing to the right with another 360 degree turn. At barrel number 3 the same passage to the right and 360 degree turn is accomplished.

Ill. 53
John's Danny, Jr. Champion Barrels, (N.M.) owned and shown by Clayborn Jones.

As soon as the turn is completed around barrel 3, the contestant sprints the horse to the finish line where the timers stop their watches as soon as the horse's nose reaches the finish line.

This barrel course may also be run to the left. For example, the contestant will start to barrel number 2, turning to left around this barrel, then to barrel number 1, turning to the right, then to barrel number 3, turning again to the right, followed by the final sprint to the finish line.

This cloverleaf pattern is designed to test the speed and maneuverabiliy of the horse. When measuring the area for the barrel course, remember to leave ample room for the horse and rider to complete their turns and also to pull to a stop at the finish.

It takes many long slow hours to develop a top barrel racing horse, for that matter a horse for any of the timed events. As in any event some horses have a knack and will watch a barrel as a cutting horse watches a cow. Other horses have to be drilled incessant hours before that particular timed event comes easy for them. The best working horses are those that can make a "run" almost on their own, working themselves there is less loss of time by excess motion or checking — excess spurring, whipping and reining invariably causes loss of time due to conflict between horse and rider.

POLE BENDING CONTEST
(This class receives half points.)

No horse shall be allowed to show in more than one approved AQHA registered pole bending contest per show.

The pole bending patten is to be run around six poles. Each pole is to be twenty-one feet apart and the first pole is to be twenty-one feet from the starting line.

A horse may start either to the right or to the left of the first pole and then run the remainder of the pattern accordingly. (See pattern.)

Knocking over a pole, touching the pole with the rider's hand, or failure to follow the course shall cause disqualification.

Pole bending is a timed event. Each contestant will begin from a running start. A clearly visible starting line shall be provided. At least two watches shall be used with the average time of the watches used by the official timers to be the official time.

In the event of a tie, the horse declared the winner in the runoff must run the pattern within two seconds of its original time or the runoff must be held again.

Western type equipment must be used. Use of a hackamore or other types of bridles is the optional choice of the contestant; however, the timer or judge may prohibit the use of bits or equipment that he may consider severe.

STAKE RACE

Start by crossing center line between the upright markers, run a figure "8" around upright markers, and finish by again crossing center line.

At the first pole, the contestant may go right or left, just so the figure "8" is run.

This is a timed event. If an upright marker is knocked down, there is no time.

Upright markers are set forty feet on either side of the center line.

In conclusion, a word about horse shows. With all their color, the matchless opportunities they offer for fellowship among horsemen, the excitement of pitting one's own horse and horsemanship against all comers, there is also the sad and not infrequently met angle of disappointment. Sometimes a rider, or the rider's teacher, thinks the disappointment is unjustified.

But with shows and showing there must, of course come judges. And no two men see beauty alike, or ugliness; no two react the same to sadness or merriment. And since this is so, and since all of us are human, no two judges can see the performance of a horse or a rider in exactly the same way, nor do they read the same interpretation into the rules. A contestant must *honor* any decision given by a judge, and, if he is disappointed, he should remember that a judge's lot is never an easy one, and that by honoring a decision he does not necessarily agree with, a rider not only contributes to good horsemanship but to good sportsmanship in general.

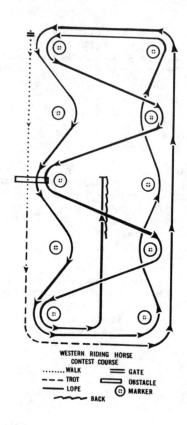

WESTERN RIDING HORSE
CONTEST COURSE

········· WALK   ═══ GATE

– – – TROT   ▬ OBSTACLE

——— LOPE   ⊕ MARKER

〰〰 BACK

LOPE OR GALLOP ———

WALK – – – – –

BACK IN STRAIGHT LINE 〰〰〰

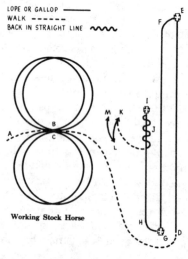

Working Stock Horse

BARREL RACING CONTEST

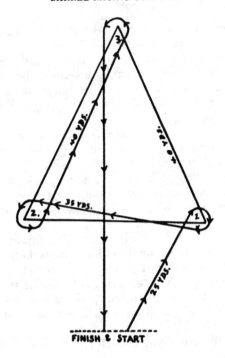

FINISH & START

POLE BENDING PATTERN

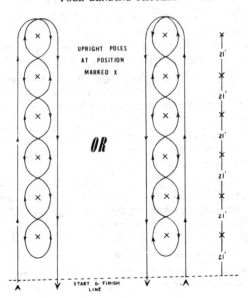

UPRIGHT POLES
AT POSITION
MARKED X

OR

21'

21'

21'

21'

21'

21'

21'

START & FINISH
LINE

Chapter XII

The horse has been trained, the rider has been trained. Now what can they do, what use is their training?

The rider has had a very thorough, painstaking course in the techniques of riding; horsemanship in general; horse-and-rider training and schooling; the teaching of riding; along with a glimpse of the responsibilities of judging. Such a rider has developed patience, tact, and physical coordination.

Individual riders will of course specialize in whatever branch of horsemanship suits them best. This might be the breaking, schooling and showing of horses; the rehabilitation of spoiled horses; or perhaps, the teaching of beginners; or the developing of horsemanship in intermediate and advanced students. The rider may do this work for pleasure, or may work for a show stable or a private stable or a dude ranch.

Or, last but not least, the rider may apply what has been learned to regular work on the ranch, thus helping to develop a better ranch horse — for it is on the ranch that the western horse began to differentiate from all other horses. The rider will get more out of his horse because of correct position and use of aids, and the horse is thus able to use itself with a minimum of strain, thus insuring its longevity.

So much for the rider. Now for the schooled horse. What can we do with him?

In him, we have the epitome of patience and controlled energy. This horse is featherlight on the rein, his understanding and obedience when he is ridden make one stand back in awe at the picture of unity he and his rider present.

Children can ride him safely because he has been taught obedience and has no fear of unjust punishment.

He can be worked on the range at top efficiency — to rope a sick calf, catch a wormy lamb, pull a reluctant heifer across the highway, cut the heavies out, or put the cows and calves through to the next pasture.

You can load him up and go to the rodeo, ride in the parade, rope calves or team-tie, whichever is his talent; your wife or your teen-ager can barrel-race on him.

Or perhaps you enter him in a quarter horse show, where he will show at halter, in the reining or western riding or pleasure classes; or your child and he will show in the junior division, in horsemanship, trail, pair or stock classes.

A teacher can use this horse in class work, to demonstrate how each movement is to be performed.

A rider for pleasure can take him on a trail ride, with a hundred other horses, or alone.

And finally, when time has caught up with him, your son, daughter, or grandchild can take over your schooled and experienced horse and learn riding from the very best of teachers. Thus, he ends his days at the most precious and exacting work of all — baby-sitting.

In that marvelous creature, your schooled horse, with faith you have established faith; from patience has come patience; from understanding, understanding has developed. From human to horse, from colt to child a feeling and spirit of unity and oneness has grown.

Only with this spirit and this feeling between the two beings can satisfaction and pleasure be gained by the human and the horse fulfill the duties and responsibilities which justify his existence in a man-made world.

AT WORK OR PLAY

In The Aren

On The Trail

In The Showrin

RAISON D' ETRE

ELVIN POWERS SELF-IMPROVEMENT LIBRARY

BUSINESS, STUDY & REFERENCE

_ BRAINSTORMING *Charles Clark*	7.00
_ CONVERSATION MADE EASY *Elliot Russell*	4.00
_ EXAM SECRET *Dennis B. Jackson*	5.00
_ FIX-IT BOOK *Arthur Symons*	2.00
_ HOW TO DEVELOP A BETTER SPEAKING VOICE *M. Hellier*	4.00
_ HOW TO SAVE 50% ON GAS & CAR EXPENSES *Ken Stansbie*	5.00
_ HOW TO SELF-PUBLISH YOUR BOOK & MAKE IT A BEST SELLER *Melvin Powers*	10.00
_ INCREASE YOUR LEARNING POWER *Geoffrey A. Dudley*	3.00
_ PRACTICAL GUIDE TO BETTER CONCENTRATION *Melvin Powers*	5.00
_ PRACTICAL GUIDE TO PUBLIC SPEAKING *Maurice Forley*	5.00
_ 7 DAYS TO FASTER READING *William S. Schaill*	5.00
_ SONGWRITERS' RHYMING DICTIONARY *Jane Shaw Whitfield*	7.00
_ SPELLING MADE EASY *Lester D. Basch & Dr. Milton Finkelstein*	3.00
_ STUDENT'S GUIDE TO BETTER GRADES *J. A. Rickard*	3.00
_ TEST YOURSELF—FIND YOUR HIDDEN TALENT *Jack Shafer*	3.00
_ YOUR WILL & WHAT TO DO ABOUT IT *Attorney Samuel G. Kling*	5.00

CHESS & CHECKERS

_ BEGINNER'S GUIDE TO WINNING CHESS *Fred Reinfeld*	5.00
_ CHESS IN TEN EASY LESSONS *Larry Evans*	5.00
_ CHESS MADE EASY *Milton L. Hanauer*	5.00
_ CHESS PROBLEMS FOR BEGINNERS *Edited by Fred Reinfeld*	5.00
_ CHESS TACTICS FOR BEGINNERS *Edited by Fred Reinfeld*	5.00
_ CHESS THEORY & PRACTICE *Morry & Mitchell*	2.00
_ HOW TO WIN AT CHECKERS *Fred Reinfeld*	5.00
_ 1001 BRILLIANT WAYS TO CHECKMATE *Fred Reinfeld*	7.00
_ 1001 WINNING CHESS SACRIFICES & COMBINATIONS *Fred Reinfeld*	7.00

HOBBIES

_ BEACHCOMBING FOR BEGINNERS *Norman Hickin*	2.00
_ BLACKSTONE'S MODERN CARD TRICKS *Harry Blackstone*	5.00
_ BLACKSTONE'S SECRETS OF MAGIC *Harry Blackstone*	5.00
_ COIN COLLECTING FOR BEGINNERS *Burton Hobson & Fred Reinfeld*	5.00
_ ENTERTAINING WITH ESP *Tony 'Doc' Shiels*	2.00
_ 400 FASCINATING MAGIC TRICKS YOU CAN DO *Howard Thurston*	5.00
_ HOW I TURN JUNK INTO FUN AND PROFIT *Sari*	3.00
_ HOW TO WRITE A HIT SONG & SELL IT *Tommy Boyce*	7.00
_ JUGGLING MADE EASY *Rudolf Dittrich*	3.00
_ MAGIC FOR ALL AGES *Walter Gibson*	4.00
_ MAGIC MADE EASY *Byron Wels*	2.00
_ STAMP COLLECTING FOR BEGINNERS *Burton Hobson*	3.00

HUMOR

_ HOW TO FLATTEN YOUR TUSH *Coach Marge Reardon*	2.00
_ HOW TO MAKE LOVE TO YOURSELF *Ron Stevens & Joy Grdnic*	3.00
_ JOKE TELLER'S HANDBOOK *Bob Orben*	7.00
_ JOKES FOR ALL OCCASIONS *Al Schock*	5.00
_ 2,000 NEW LAUGHS FOR SPEAKERS *Bob Orben*	5.00
_ 2,400 JOKES TO BRIGHTEN YOUR SPEECHES *Robert Orben*	7.00
_ 2,500 JOKES TO START 'EM LAUGHING *Bob Orben*	7.00

SELF-HELP & INSPIRATIONAL

_ CHARISMA—HOW TO GET "THAT SPECIAL MAGIC" *Marcia Grad*	7.00
_ DAILY POWER FOR JOYFUL LIVING *Dr. Donald Curtis*	7.00
_ DYNAMIC THINKING *Melvin Powers*	5.00
_ GREATEST POWER IN THE UNIVERSE *U. S. Andersen*	7.00
_ GROW RICH WHILE YOU SLEEP *Ben Sweetland*	7.00
_ GROWTH THROUGH REASON *Albert Ellis, Ph.D.*	7.00
_ GUIDE TO PERSONAL HAPPINESS *Albert Ellis, Ph.D. & Irving Becker, Ed.D.*	7.00
_ HANDWRITING ANALYSIS MADE EASY *John Marley*	7.00
_ HANDWRITING TELLS *Nadya Olyanova*	7.00
_ HOW TO ATTRACT GOOD LUCK *A.H.Z. Carr*	7.00
_ HOW TO BE GREAT *Dr. Donald Curtis*	5.00

The books listed above can be obtained from your book dealer or directly from Melvin Power
When ordering, please remit $1.50 postage for the first book and 50¢ for each additional book

Melvin Powers
12015 Sherman Road, No. Hollywood, California 91605